The Sacred Word

Helen C. Watling

www.capallbann.co.uk

The Sacred Word

ISBN 186163 109X

Cover design by Paul Mason
Internal illustrations by Helen Watling

Published by:

Capall Bann Publishing
Freshfields
Chieveley
Berks
RG20 8TF

Contents

Introduction 1

Chapter One Sound, Speech and Symbol 5

Chapter Two On Stone and Papyrus 18

Chapter Three In the Beginning....... 46

Chapter Four Word-Masters and Wood-Sages 75

Chapter Five The Gift of Hermes 112

Chapter Six Runic Wisdom 139

Chapter Seven In the Realm of Magic Esoteric Alphabets 175

Chapter Eight Influences 185

Chapter Nine Sacred Inspiration 193

Bibliography 201

Index 203

Introduction

Language is something that most of us take for granted. When we speak or write in our everyday lives we do not think of these gifts as in any way miraculous or magical, or about what life would be like without language, without the spoken or the written word.

Pause for a moment and try to imagine..........

How would your thought processes operate without words, without that continuous monologue which runs in your head as you go through the day? How does language affect your understanding of the world? Your relationships with others? Your fantasies?

Words - sound vibrations or symbols seen on a page - have the power to describe images in the mind, or to create them and to evoke whole inner worlds. This happens every time we read a novel or poem, or hear a description. If someone tells us about a place thousands of miles away or perhaps one which flourished thousands of years ago, we feel as if we can see the architecture, hear the sea and smell the perfume of exotic flowers. What is this but magic?

It is a magic that has been recognized by humans since the earliest times, though belief in the word as the primary creative force is a product of later patriarchal religions. Originally it was believed that a mother goddess gave birth to the world, whereas language is a medium through which men (and gods) as well as women can 'give birth'. It is a left brain function, associated with logical so-called 'masculine' thought, but through language 'feminine' right brain vision and imagination can be expressed. As a man impregnates a woman and she gives birth, so the muse

1

- or goddess, who is never directly mentioned in the patriarchal myths - impregnates the minds of male creator deities with inspiration, causing them to speak the first creative words.

The god of the Hebrews not only spoke the word that brought about creation but, according to the Bible, he was the word, the Logos. And Qabalistic belief, based on Hebrew holy books, states that the true name of the biblical god is too powerful to be spoken aloud except by high initiates.

The word created, but could also destroy. Sound vibrations have been used to heal, to bring harmony as in the case of the eastern mantra Om, or to cause disintegration. It is well known that a trained singer hitting a certain note can make a glass shatter. Because human beings, like all other 'solid' objects, are made up of atoms we are affected by sound frequencies, vibrations, which cause changes in the forces which bind these atoms together.

Though this book is primarily about the word, in its spoken form it cannot be seen in isolation from music, song and chant, as all three produce vibration. They can change states of consciousness and bring dramatic changes in emotion. In the case of songs, the word-pictures add to the combination of notes and rhythm to affect listeners, as the ancient Celtic Bards well knew. Years of intense training gave them great power over an audience, the ability to make them switch from anger to grief at the sound of a few carefully chosen notes and evocative words. People's emotions, and also their mental and physical well-being, were in the power of the druidic Bards who could bless or curse. The Celts believed that not only humans, but nature spirits, deities, and the land itself could be similarly affected.

So the vibration of sound has incredible power, but what about symbols? Though the letters of our own alphabet are used every day on a mundane level they possess as much hidden potency as a cross, a pentagram or an ankh. And there is an interesting link between sound and symbol.

Research has shown that various sound combinations cause unique vibrational patterns, ie. symbols. In the eighteenth century a German, Ernst Chladni, discovered that sand placed on a metal disc formed into patterns when notes were played on a violin. The reason, he found, was that the disc only vibrated in certain places, causing the sand to move to those areas which did not vibrate. Therefore, the part of the pattern where there was no sand represented the true symbol for that particular sound.

Inspired by Chladni's work, a man named Hans Jenny invented a machine called a tonoscope which showed the pattern of various sounds on a screen. He found that when the mantra Om was correctly vibrated it created geometric shapes, a circle containing further circles and triangles. Order is created out of chaos, reminiscent of the biblical creation myth.

If we recite the alphabet each letter has its own vibrational pattern, and though early alphabets are thought to have derived from pictorial representations of objects, could their inventors have had an awareness of what Ernst Chladni (re?)discovered thousands of years later?

Probably all alphabets were once used only for magico-religious purposes, before being put to secular use, and in many ancient cultures priests and few others were literate.

Throughout the millenia, from Dynastic Egypt to Medieval Europe letters, incantations, names and words played a vital role, first in religion, which had a strongly magical bias, and later in the occult arts, after Christianity had driven magic underground. Words we still use today illustrate the ancient links. Grammar and grimoire - a book of magical rites and spells - both derive from gramaire, learning, and the two meanings of the word 'spell' give a clue to its original dual interpretation.

With a few exceptions the cultures dealt with in this book come under what is commonly referred to as the Western Mystery Tradition, though the principles apply worldwide. And, as I hope I have shown, the effects of symbol and sound are as powerful

3

now as for the ancient Egyptian priests or the Norse runemasters.

Invocation, chants, talismans, and divination are only a few of the modern applications for the sacred word, showing how the magical use of alphabets can bring about change in our lives. Also, though initially these may not seem to be connected with magic, poetry and fiction play an important role.

As you read each word of this, or any other book, you are performing a magical act, giving black symbols on a white background a colourful tapestry of meaning. The rite has already begun........

Chapter One

Sound, Speech and Symbol

Once upon a time, as hominids travelled the long road from ape-man to technological wizard, they developed the miracle of using language. This, along with the ability to walk upright on two legs, differentiated our species from other animals. It brought about untold possibilities for progress on all levels, pushing us yet further ahead in the survival game and eventually leading to overall world domination.

Around 40,000 years ago the race of *Homo sapiens* made its appearance, replacing *Homo erectus*, the discoverer of fire, who in turn had replaced *Homo habilis*, the first tool user. *Homo erectus* existed for over a million years, spreading from Africa to Asia, the Middle East and Europe. This race was successful and relatively highly developed, yet it finally gave way to one still more intelligent, who in turn colonized the world.

When our direct ancestors first began to evolve, perhaps 30,000 years earlier, they still had some way to go. Though they had large brains, weighing the same as those of humans today, they lacked an ego, the consciousness of individuality. Nor did they have a concept of past and future as we would understand them. They could make simple, short-term plans, such as shaping a stone axe and taking it out on a hunting expedition, but could not think months ahead or go beyond the basic skills needed for survival. At least, not until they developed the ability to use language in a sophisticated way.

It may well have been the use of language that led them to displace their predecessor, *Homo erectus*, who lacked this most valuable and unique skill. That is not to say that *Homo erectus*, the earlier Home habilis, and extinct races of ape-man such as the Neanderthal were unable to use simple verbal communication, involving a system of grunts, gestures and facial expressions.

In early humans, as today, eye contact would have been important, and a great deal could be said by attracting another person's attention to an object by looking at it then using appropriate sounds or gestures. For example, glancing at a joint of meat and making friendly noises would say 'help yourself'. An angry look or grunt could also warn another person that his or her behaviour was unwelcome. But the situations in these examples are very immediate, there has to be an object for both parties to look at, or an action taking place at that moment, for one person to understand the other. There is a vast gap between this kind of communication and what could be termed true language.

Language is a set of sounds with symbolic meanings. Each sound made does not have to relate to an object that is visible or to an event which is happening at the time, though this is how it must have originated. Early humans, living in closely knit social groups for the purposes of hunting, gathering and rearing children, had to develop good communication in the group as a part of the social skills needed for survival. Gradually, certain sounds - words - developed meanings understood by the whole group and were passed down from generation to generation, each adding more words.

The 'words' used at this stage would have been more like grunts than what we now understand as words. They would probably have had a general rather than a specific meaning and would not have been part of a grammatical sentence, but rather uttered singly or with a few related sounds following each other. Besides not having developed a complicated vocabulary, early humans did not have the physical capacity to speak as we do today. The reason we can make so many varied sounds is the curved roof of our mouths, mobile tongue, strong throat muscles and firm lips, and the fact that our voice boxes have moved far down the throat.

Archaeological discoveries of human remains show that an arched palate first appeared in the skulls of *Homo erectus* about 1.5 million years ago, though at this stage the arch was not pronounced. Only *Homo sapiens* possessed the right shape of palate to form words as we do today.

As evolution continued, changes to the lips, tongue and throat enabled human beings to speak more quickly and efficiently, as did changes to the areas of the brain which affected these parts. We need to be able to speak reasonably fast or, because of limited short term memory, we would forget the beginning of a long sentence before it was finished, making it impossible to understand the overall meaning. Unlike *Homo erectus*, who had poorly developed speech mechanisms and who could only utter a word a second, *Homo sapiens* had the opportunity of developing more complicated sentences rather than basic disjointed grunts.

Homo sapiens also had a brain nearly twice the size of *Homo ereceus;* giving extra capacity for language. The left side of our brain is connected with this faculty, while areas located behind the left ear deal specifically with the power of speech.

Finally, humans had evolved the physical and mental capacities for true language, though they had yet to begin forming flowing grammatical sentences. As the understanding of purely symbolic words could not be aided by gestures, instead mankind had to learn how to clarify them by uttering further symbolic words in a logical order. Our distant ancestors slowly invented the earliest forms of grammar, which would have reflected the way they viewed life, probably similar to our subject, verb and object, showing how each person actively affected and interacted with the surrounding environment.

Of course all the beneficial side-effects of language did not appear overnight, but were a product of cultural evolution over thousands of years. However, human beings had developed a skill which offered new dimensions of awareness.

The main change brought about by the development of language was that humans were freed from the trap of living only in the present moment. With symbolic words a person gained access to his or her inner landscape. Dreams and mental pictures obviously existed before language, but now every object in that inner world could be called up by the utterance of the correct sound, and not only pictorial objects but imagination, emotion, memory and long-term plans for the future.

The power of language gave birth to the self, the ego, an individual mind as separate from the group mind of the tribe. A child was, and still is, brought up to be a part of society, conforming to its conventions, but we are also taught a sense of self-identity, largely enshrined in words.

Early humans would at some point have developed an equivalent to the word 'I' and, like a toddler today learning to use this word, gained a name for their sense of self-awareness which could then be developed, reinforced by personal memory and imagination.

Without language human beings, and other animals, can of course feel pleasure, pain, hunger, sex urges etc, and have an awareness of the external world. But after the evolution of reasonably advanced speech they could also step outside themselves and the present moment, turning outer awareness round to analyse the inner realm of their thoughts and feelings.

As people's thought processes sharpened their horizons extended in all directions: physical, mental and spiritual. Driven by that curiousity which is a part of our nature, certain tribes embarked on a great adventure, setting out for areas far distant from their original homelands, involving travel over large tracts of water, a feat which no one had previously attempted.

And once human beings were self-aware they began to ask deep and increasingly complex questions about themselves and the world around them, which in turn brought awe mingled with fear. What mighty powers lay behind all existence, putting the stars in the heavens, regulating the cycle of the seasons, the phases of the moon, giving life but claiming it again, often violently and prematurely? And where did a person's spirit go when it left the body at death?

The world was filled with unfathomable mysteries. 40,000 years ago, as now, there were questions which could not be answered with certainty. Yet we have always tried to give order to chaos, to comprehend the incomprehensible.

The naming of an object, idea or feeling brought it into greater focus than in the days before language. Once something was named it gained an identity, it became clearly differentiated from other things and could be discussed, compared and remembered. As objects and ideas acquired important associations beliefs and customs developed, including rules for society and magical taboos.

For the first time people could conceive of gods and spirits, they could give a name and attributes to what had previously been no more than shadowy dreams, intuitive feelings and fears about nature.That which had no definite existence in people's awareness before language now became real for them. Man created the gods in his own image rather than the other way around, as the Hebrew god of the Old Testament is said to have done. Though it would be more true to say that early deities were created in woman's image, as all the first sculptures, presumed to be goddesses, are of the female form. But before these could be modelled, an inner vision must have existed .

By naming spiritual, invisible forces men and women also formed a link with them. In a sense they captured part of the force within the name. Each time the god name was used the link was re-established.

As with deities, so with objects and people. Early humans would have so closely identified the thing with its name that the two were linked by more than merely symbolic association. In many ancient cultures, as in some American Indian and Australian aborigine tribes, a person's name was regarded as a vital part of their self, as much so as their nails or hair. Because of this there was a taboo on revealing a person's 'real' or magical name, and another name had to be used in secular life.

Names and words have power. The fact was recognized from the birth of language, giving rise to myth and magico-religious observance. And, naturally, words were also an invaluable tool in day to day existence, enabling humans both to improve their minds and their lifestyle.

But even with the phenomenon of the spoken word now well established amongst early peoples the story of language had only just begun. So far the word could only be retained in memory and passed down from mouth to ear. A more permanent method of recording both trade transactions and sacred lore was lacking. Not content with simply observing, *Homo sapiens* had been inspired to make three dimensional figurines as early as 30,000 BC, probably for magical and religious purposes. These, as mentioned earlier, were of crude female figures, one of the best known being the so-called Venus of Willendorf, found in Austria and dated to approximately 20,000 BC. By this time humans had also mastered the art of two- dimensional drawing, shown in many beautiful cave paintings like the mare from Lascaux cave in the Dordogne, France, created around 15,000 BC.

Early religious artists did not only portray complete figures of animals or goddesses, but they also used symbols to convey an idea without having to draw the full picture. The symbol of an inverted triangle carved in the pubic area of goddess figurines is shown in an early example (c. 30,000 BC) from Mezin, western Ukraine, and on the 'Lady of Pazardzik', which is later (c. 4500 BC) and more realistic in form. The meaning of this symbol, associated with the goddess and fertility/re-birth, would have been understood by pre-historic peoples from Russia to Ireland, even when it was no longer carved on a figurine but, for example, on the kerbstones of the Neolithic passage grave at Newgrange, Ireland.

Other wide-spread pre-historic symbols are the spiral, the circle, the lozenge, the wavy line/zigzag and the chevron. A lozenge with a dot in the centre is thought te stand for a field containing a seed, or could also represent a vulva, and is found carved on the stomach of a figure from Yugoslavia dated to around 6000 BC, again indicating the fertility of the goddess.

The spiral, often engraved in conjunction with the triangle and lozenge, would have been observed by early humans as occuring in nature, on the snail's shell and in whirlpools. It perfectly evokes the continuous cycles of life: birth, death and rebirth, just as the seasons turn and no end is final, only the start of a new cycle. The circle would have had a similar meaning of continuity, and also of completeness.

These examples show how pictorial symbolism was developing as early as the Palaeolithic or old stone age, symbols closely related to the most archaic forms of writing. One such symbol, seen on a 20,000 year old bracelet of mammoth ivory from the Ukraine and on the lintels of the Neolithic passage tomb at Fourknocks, Southern Ireland, is the wavy line or zigzag, representing the waters of life needed to fertilize the earth mother. This same zigzag was the symbol for water in both Chinese and Egyptian hieroglyphic writing.

Besides the symbols mentioned above many more exist. Some of the earliest linear symbols date from around 12,000 BC, painted with red ocre on a mammoth skull from the Ukraine.

With the dawn of the Neolithic era or new stone age people gradually adopted a more settled lifestyle, and farming took the place of the earlier hunter-gatherer and nomadic herd-raising cultures. Growing crops meant that a far smaller area of land could support a larger number of people as the population increased. It also meant a greater need for keeping records and

1. Kerbstone K67 from Newgrange Neolithic passage grave, Southern Ireland. The engravings could represent a spell for abundance, the two lozenges indicating the Goddess' fertility placed at the meeting point between the spirals of life and death.

tallies of produce. Both written numbers and letters were needed.

Clay was used for this purpose in the Middle East. Originally stones representing quantities were sealed in clay balls, with marks indicating the contents scratched on the outside. But before long people realized that the stones were superfluous, and instead started to inscribe flat tablets of clay.

In Old Europe - an area covering much of eastern and southern Europe - an advanced town-based civilization flourished around 5000 BC, possessing its own script which can be found on artefacts such as figurines, spindle whorls and vessels. Some of its characters bear a resemblance to those of the much later runic letters, and recognizable symbols like the cross and swastika are also found.

Most ancient scripts developed from pictograms representing something seen in nature or created by humans; while numbers consisted of tally strokes, often accompanied by a pictogram to indicate what had been counted. As civilization advanced, and in Old Europe and the Middle East increasing numbers of people lived in towns rather than in isolated farmsteads, writing became ever more important in religious and secular life, but it still remained a secret held only by the few. To the mass of the population the art of translating rows of symbols into comprehensible words was mysterious and awe-inspiring.

As time passed the symbols became less and less like the original pictures, and many words had no obvious image to represent them in the first place. A scribe could no more draw a literal symbol for each word than earlier man could point at everything he wished to discuss. The whole process had advanced to the next sweep of the ever-turning spiral. As letters and words were simplified in appearance greater knowledge was needed to understand them.

It is impossible to know what the language of the Neolithic peoples was like as they left no written record. The only possible

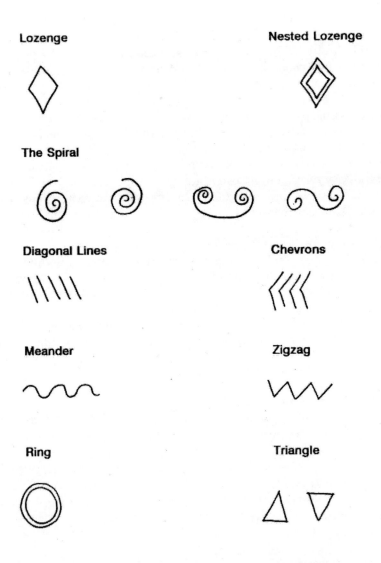

Some of the main symbols which occur in Neolithic art

clue lies in the Basque tongue, found in the Pyrenees. This is unrelated to any other known language, and spoken by a people who are thought to descend from the Neolithic inhabitants of Europe.

Even with cultures who did leave documentary evidence, such as the Egyptians, we cannot tell how their language was spoken, with what accent, emphasis and inflection. Other ancient scripts which could, and hopefully one day will, tell us more about the civilizations which gave them birth still have not been deciphered - that of Old Europe and of the Minoan culture from Crete, both an influence on the later classical Greek world.

Before 3500 BC peoples speaking what is now referred to as the Indo-European mother tongue lived in an area around central Europe and southern Russia. Though they need not necessarily have been the same ethnically, they shared the same language, which they took across both Europe and Asia when they migrated.

Those who travelled south east to India brought with them a language which developed into Sanskrit, the language of the *Vedas* or sacred books. Others travelled west into Europe, their language giving rise to Greek, Latin, Germanic (from which English derives) and Celtic. Iranian, Armenian, Albanian, Balto-Slavic, Hittite and Tocharian also share the same roots. The two latter, belonging to long since extinct civilizations, are known only from texts discovered this century - the Hittite in Asia Minor, ninety miles from Ankara, the Tocharian in Chinese Turkestan.

Clues to the links between these diverse languages were first noticed in the eighteenth century by Sir William Jones, a British judge living in India, whose theories were fully developed in the early nineteenth century.

An example of what Jones noticed is shown by the similarity of the word for father in eight different Indo-European languages, though the ancient mother tongue has long since faded into oblivion: English -father, Dutch - vader, Gothic - fadar, Old Norse - fabir, German - vater, Greek - pater, Sanskrit- pitar, and Old Irish - athir.

The *Vedas* give us the earliest written example of an Indo-European language, the oldest text dating from around 1500 BC. As with most early writings those in Sanskrit focus on religious and magical belief, and only later did it gain a wider scope. Today Sanskrit is still studied as a religious language, though it has not been in common use since ancient times.

Babylonian (Akkadian) and Hebrew are classed as Semetic languages, and ancient Egyptian is in a class by itself. However, the other scripts to be dealt with in this book are all from the Indo-European group, and all have had a connection with the British Isles and an influence either on our language or our alphabet, and in some cases both.

The Celtic language is still spoken in Wales, and in Ireland and Scotland as Gaelic. It is also found in some English place names, especially in Cornwall and the south west, for example tor, creech, pen and combe. As is fitting for a culture which lived in close contact with nature, most of the Celtic names are attached to natural features of the landscape.

Even after the Roman conquest in 43 AD Celtic would have been used throughout the country, and only a small proportion of the population learnt to speak Latin. It was the language of officialdom, of the wealthy, used in its written form for inscriptions and public records.

Our modern English language is of west Germanic origin, brought from Europe by the Angles, Saxons and Jutes who gradually occupied the British Isles after 449 AD. Some of these settlers would have been familiar with the runic system, using it for Pagan religious and magical purposes, as well as for inscriptions and dedications. Then, with the conversion to Christianity from 597 onwards, the Latin alphabet returned, and a way had to be found of adapting it to write English words. Though, as in the Pagan world, literacy was still largely the province of those involved in religion, and the monks who produced the long beautifully illuminated manuscripts of the period not only wrote with the Latin alphabet but also in the Latin tongue.

It is through our daily use of the Latin alphabet that we find our link with the Greek alphabet from which it derives. English gained elements of Latin through contact with the Roman civilization in Europe before the Germanic tribes left the Continent and from Romanized Celts, but mainly through the influence of the church and as a result of the Norman conquest. Norman French is a Romance language, based on Latin.

No living language is ever static, but always developing, evolving. The complete story of the word will never be written because as long as humankind survives on this earth language will grow with us, individually and as a species. To each of us our way of speech is as unique as our physical appearance, and a magical tool carried with us at all times.

Language gives us a window on our own selves, and a key to powerful hidden dimensions. The mysteries of the word are no less sacred now because they are no longer jealously guarded for use only by priests and scribes. And the legends through which ancient peoples sought to understand what they sensed to be true still have a great deal to say if we listen with an open mind.

Chapter Two

On Stone and Papyrus

At a time before time nothing existed but the ocean of chaos, called Nun. Out of this nothingness a thought arose, and the thought uttered the name Ptah. And so the first god came into being, self-created. Now Ptah, who still existed alone in the nothingness, thought of solid earth and spoke its name, causing the primeval mound to rise from the waters. At his word each thing in heaven or on earth materialized: the powerful gods, the firmament with all its stars, and all living beings: plant, animal and human.

For the ancient Egyptians the word was sacred, over and above anything else, because without the word they believed there would have been no existence. Likewise, if a magician knew and understood how to pronounce the words of power there were no limits to what s/he could create, alter or destroy. The world revolved around names and words and magic. This terrifying power was contained within the symbolic characters of the hieroglphic alphabet, linking what was visible and tangible with the unseen dimensions.

The culture which lived by these beliefs was one of the oldest in the west, and one which still holds a unique place in the hearts of many people for its art and architecture, but more than anything for its religion.

Historical Background
The Egyptian civilization had its beginnings along the banks of the Nile during the Palaeolithic era, when hunter-gatherers first

built their camp sites near the river, making the most of the fish, game and vegetation which abounded.

The most recent remains belonging to this period date to around 10,000 BC, though all physical evidence representing the following five thousand years is as yet undiscovered. After the millenia which still hide their secrets in the Nile mud, the first evidence to come to light shows that a major advance had been made; the early Egyptians had progressed into the Neolithic age. Life now revolved around cultivation and animal rearing, with pottery-making, weaving and basketry also practised. Existence was primitive and simple, similar to a comparable period in European pre-history, and writing was as yet unknown.

Then, at around 3500 BC, a rapid advance towards civilization took place when the indiginous peoples came into contact with others from western Asia, through trade and immigration. These more sophisticated societies introduced the Egyptians to the technique for building with sun-dried mud bricks, stamping clay with cyclinder seals and creating new styles of ornamentation. The above developments coincided with the first attempts at pictographic writing, probably inspired by the Mesopotamian Jemdet Nasr culture which had reached Syria by the late fourth millenium BC.

However, advance did not bring stability. In the second half of the millenium internal strife between Upper and Lower Egypt, combined with external threats from neighbouring lands, led to a state of anarchy where no further progress could be made. A strong leader was needed to restore order, and in answer to this need, according to classical authors, a man named Menes took control, establishing a union between the two lands of Egypt. He became the first pharaoh of a unified kingdom around 3150 BC, ending the pre-dynastic period.

Traditionally Menes founded the city of 'White Walls', later known as Memphis, of which Ptah became the patron deity. Just as Menes built his new capital on land reclaimed from the Nile, Ptah created the primeval mound from the waters of chaos.

Creation Myths

The story of the creation by the god Ptah will probably seem strangely familiar, even to readers who have no knowledge of Egyptian myth. The fact that Ptah, chief god of Memphis, brings the world into being by the same means as the god of the Bible illustrates how ancient cultures frequently revered the word as the giver of life. Though, as different areas of Egypt worshipped their own deities, and in various periods of history different pantheons rivalled each other for prominence, there are numerous creation myths, not all of which involve the sacred word.

Of those that do, some state that it was Thoth, god of Hermopolis, who spoke the words which brought the world into being. When he became conscious of himself in the primeval waters of chaos he opened his mouth and uttered a sound, and from that sound first four gods, then four goddesses materialized. These eight deities continued Thoth's work of creation by means of the word, and sang hymns at the beginning and end of each day to ensure that the sun continued on its course. Another version states that only after Thoth spoke the creative words was Ptah endowed with the energy to manifest the universe.

A tale of creation similar to that involving Ptah, in which a generally unknown deity speaks the words, is found in the Papyrus of Nesi-Amsu. The god Neb-er-tcher says, "I brought (i.e. made) my mouth, and I uttered my own name as a word of power, and thus I evolved myself under the evolutions of the god Khepera, and I developed myself out of the primeval matter which had evolved multitudes of evolutions from the beginning of time. Nothing existed on this earth (before me), I made all things.'

Alternatively it was the god Khepera who created himself from the primeval matter by uttering his own name, which means 'he who becomes'. As god of the sun at midnight, he represents transformation, rebirth and potentiality, all symbolic of the continuity of creation.

On a physical level it is impossible to speak without exhaling, so each word is fuelled by vital breath, in a sense with its own life. When this is linked with the fact that all matter consists of vibration, and that sound produces vibration which can form patterns, the Egyptian creation myths show more than symbolic relevance.

Ptah

Written in hieroglyphic characters.

The Memphite creator god is depicted with his body bound in mummy wrappings and a tight-fitting skull cap covering his head. Only his fore-arms, hands and face are visible. His name, meaning 'force captured in form', describes his creative energy, and is also linked to his mummified image. Though Ptah's movements are restricted by the wrappings, as the spirit is temporarily chained by incarnation, both retain their power.

In the theology of ancient Memphis all living things were said to have been created by Ptah's heart and tongue, the former as the seat of intellect, the latter representing the commands he uttered. Besides being the deity who spoke the words of creation Ptah's generative powers extended to craftsmanship, making him the patron of builders and masons. He was known as the Architect of the Universe, a title still used by modern Freemasons with reference to a supreme being.

In statues and paintings Ptah is shown holding the 'was' sceptre, representing dominion. The upper portion of the sceptre comprises the ankh, symbol of eternal life, combined with the djed column, symbol of stability, illustrating the god's ability to create and sustain life.

During funerary rites the officiating setem-priest represented Ptah as he performed the ceremony of 'opening the mouth' on the mummified body or on a statue of the deceased. This ceremony was standard procedure, and involved symbolically opening the mouth of the deceased by placing an adze with a flint or iron

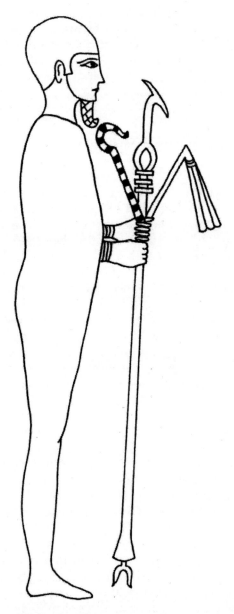

Ptah, the Creator

blade against the lips in order to restore life, which would then endure for ever, provided the tomb had been equipped correctly and the correct offerings were still made after the funeral rites were over. 'Opening the mouth' also restored all its functions such as breathing, eating and speaking, the latter being vitally important in order to speak the words of power that would ensure survival in the Afterworld.

As the creator, Ptah was the first to perform this ceremony in the beginning of time when he granted life to the gods. The implement he used was a metal chisel, linking in with his role as the patron deity of masons.

Interestingly, Ptah is partnered with the lion-headed destroyer goddess Sekhmet, making the point that all which is created must also perish in the ever-turning cycle of being.

Thoth - Lord of Sacred Words

Another major deity associated with uttering the words of creation from amidst the ocean of chaos was Thoth, supreme god of magic. As inventor and patron of all learning and wisdom and all the arts and sciences, he presided over astronomy, geometry, mathematics, music, painting, soothsaying, surgery, surveying and medicine, as well as magic.

Thoth, the Greek form of the Egyptian Djeheuty or Tehuti, written as shown, was a lunar deity depicted as either an ibis-headed man, an ibis or a baboon. He wears a crown representing the crescent moon supporting the full moon disc, sometimes also decorated with a feather, emblem of divine truth and justice.

Known as the Lord of Sacred Words, he was believed to have shown the Egyptians how to write using hieroglyphs, therefore endowing the letters with magical potency. The ancient Egyptians called their alphabet 'medu neter', meaning 'words of the god'.

3. Thoth, Lord of Sacred Words

Literacy was a rare talent, as only the children of wealthy families were taught to read and write in the first place, and then they did not necessarily cultivate the skill in daily use. It required a good memory and a great deal of patience to remember and apply over 500 characters.

This meant that the profession of scribe was one of honour and privilege, receiving and preserving the sacred wisdom. They regarded Thoth as their patron deity, and every morning a scribe would make an offering to him by sprinkling the ground with water from the bowl used to mix writing inks.

The scribes' role was so exclusive that they were even exempt from paying taxes, and they held positions of great responsibility, such as managing the temple libraries with their collections of priceless secret documents. An example is the legendary Per Ankh, meaning House of Life, a library of papyri only accessible to scribes, which housed such works as medical manuals, mathematical treatises and documents on etiquette, said to be under the divine protection of Thoth.

Thoth himself was scribe to the gods, and is depicted carrying an 'ink' palette and reed brush as the symbols of his craft. Because he was regarded as faultlessly honest and impartial Thoth judged divine disputes, including the contest between Horus and Seth, in which he ruled in favour of the former.

Another of his roles was as patron of history, keeping a written record of all that occured in the realm of the gods and of humans, such as listing the succession of kings. It was also his duty to list all the souls who entered the Underworld, known as Duat.

He possessed great eloquence, to the extent that his very voice had magical properties. It is recorded that his words were sufficient to end aggression in the land of Egypt.

In Osiris' judgement chamber, the Hall of Two Truths, where the heart of a dead person was weighed against a the feather of truth to decide whether they deserved reward or punishment, Thoth

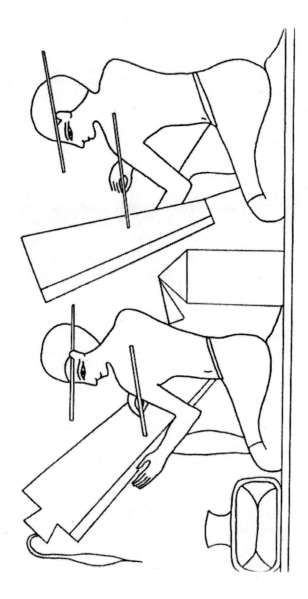

4. Egyptian scribes at work.

was in charge of the balance and stood ready with his writing equipment to record the result. He was then responsible for reporting this result to Osiris. If the deceased had committed no sins he was described as 'true of voice', indicating the sacred nature of speech.

The temple of Esna contained an inscription: 'Djeheuty pa aa, pa aa, pa aa', translated as 'Thoth the great, the great, the great', so that when the early Greeks identified Hermes, their god of letters, with the Egyptian deity who had similar attributes they came up with the title Hermes Trismegistos. By this name he was revered by occultists from ancient to Medieval times, and on to the present day. (See Chapters 5 and 7).

The Story of Hieroglyphics

The sacred letters which were Thoth's gift to humankind were used throughout Egyptian history prior to the Roman conquest, evolving, as time passed, through three phases. The oldest of these three forms of writing was the hieroglphic system, where the characters took the form of pictograms, accurately portraying the objects represented. They were cut in stone or wood with copper, bronze or iron chisels, producing precise, clear-cut results. The characters were then painted according to convention. For example, celestial features, metal containers and instruments were blue; the natural world was shown in its true colours; and an Egyptian man was red, a woman yellow or pinkish-brown. However, by no means all artist-scribes adhered to the conventions, and many characters were coloured as their whim, or paint supply, dictated.

Hieroglyphs can be written in vertical columns or in horizontal lines, some reading from right to left, others vice versa. Though this may sound confusing the reader only has to look to see which direction any animals, birds or people are facing and then read towards them.

At an early date the ancient Egyptians discovered yet another material on which to write.......papyrus, made from the stalk of a

Giving the meanings of the letters as ideographs or determinatives

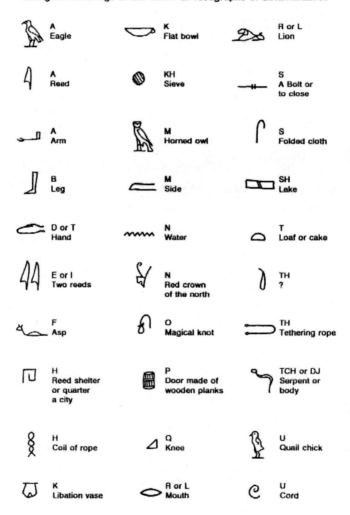

A Eagle	**K** Flat bowl	**R or L** Lion
A Reed	**KH** Sieve	**S** A Bolt or to close
A Arm	**M** Horned owl	**S** Folded cloth
B Leg	**M** Side	**SH** Lake
D or T Hand	**N** Water	**T** Loaf or cake
E or I Two reeds	**N** Red crown of the north	**TH** ?
F Asp	**O** Magical knot	**TH** Tethering rope
H Reed shelter or quarter a city	**P** Door made of wooden planks	**TCH or DJ** Serpent or body
H Coil of rope	**Q** Knee	**U** Quail chick
K Libation vase	**R or L** Mouth	**U** Cord

The Hieroglyphic Alphabet

plant which grew plentifully beside the Nile. Papyrus, a Greek word from which our own word paper derives, had a great advantage in that it was light and portable, and scrolls could be used for trade transactions and lengthy official documents. The only drawback was that the characters could not be as well defined as when cut with a chisel.

The scribes writing on papyrus used a reed pen, or more accurately a brush, the end having been crushed to make the fibres flexible. For ink they used vegetable colourings or coloured earths blended with water and gum.

As the use of papyrus increased over a period of time and writing was employed for official purposes, with less scope for artistry, the pictograms became less recognizable as objects and instead degenerated into more abstract symbols. The script which resulted is known as hieratic, which was usually read in horizontal lines from right to left, though it is occasionally found in columns.

Much later, c. 900 BC, the hieratic characters were simplified yet again, becoming the purely abstract demotic script. As the evolution of Egyptian writing from the earliest periods has been so well preserved it shows us the route all other written characters must have taken as they developed, though in most cases the evidence has been lost.

Finally, the Coptic dialect and its accompanying script came into use in the second century AD, though Greek letters rather than Egyptian demotic characters formed its alphabet. with six characters derived from demotic added to express sounds which did not occur in Greek.

Coptic is basically a form of the ancient Egyptian language, and as such indicates how the ancient tongue was spoken, despite inevitable changes brought about by the passage of time. It is found mainly in Christian literature and is still used in the religious rites of the Coptic Christian Church, though it has not been spoken in secular life since about the fifteenth century.

Being able to read hieroglyphic characters has given us access to a wealth of information about ancient Egyptian life, from day to day affairs, politics and trade to religious belief. For this we owe a debt to a Frenchman named Jean François Champollion (1790-1832), a formidable linguist and scholar who found the key to deciphering the hieroglyphic system, opening the door on lost knowledge. He accomplished the feat with the aid of the Rosetta Stone, a large piece of basalt found by a soldier in the Napoleonic army during the French invasion of Egypt, which was inscribed with the same text in Greek, and in the demotic and hieroglyphic scripts.

The writing and reading of hieroglyphics is an extremely complicated discipline, as each picture can stand for a number of things, abstract or concrete. On the simplest level the characters are ideographs, representing the thing pictured, for example the symbol shown top right means an eagle. Secondly, a character could represent an abstract idea associated with the picture, such as a musical instrument (bottom) meaning pleasure, joy and goodness. Each letter, therefore, had a name, ie. of the object or idea it represented, as is the case with the letters of Hebrew alphabet, though the shape of the Hebrew letters no longer resemble the actual objects after which they were named.

Because only simple texts could be written just with ideographs, the ancient Egyptians also used certain signs to express syllables or single letters, such as this standing for the syllable 'maat'.

As with the Hebrew alphabet, single letters were derived from the initial letter of the object depicted, for example represents the letter M. The hieroglyph shows a horned owl, mûlotch in Coptic.

Besides being used alone to represent an object, ideographs were also used as determinatives. These were placed at the end of a word to clarify its meaning, which was not always obvious once symbols representing letters and syllables were employed. For example if a word had two or more possible meanings an ideograph would indicate the relevant one.

With hundreds of characters to be mastered the hieroglphic script was not the most practical way of writing, and only the select few were literate. However, the very fact that being able to read or write the characters was the result of a lengthy period of study only added to their sacred value. They were not a tool to be placed in the hands of the profane as their power was such that they could prove dangerous if not treated with the greatest reverence.

The Magic of Words and Hieroglyphs

To the ancient Egyptians letters were so much more than simply the component parts of words, and hieroglphic characters contained many layers of esoteric meaning. Besides being letters, some also figure as religious symbols associated with deities, for example:

The Ankh

One of the most well-known signs, the ankh, often figures in artistic representations and is frequently held by a god or goddess. Not only does it stand for the word 'life' but also for the syllable 'ankh'. It is composed of the symbol above a tau cross.

stands for the letter 'r' as a single alphabetic letter, or as a pictogram for an opening, a mouth, a door, birth, or a uterus. As a mouth it can be linked with speech, seen as a creative life-giving gift in association with Ptah and Khepera. These gods 'gave birth' through the word, as the new-born child emerges from the uterus, hence both the mouth and the uterus are the door to life.

Similarly the ankh can be seen as the circle of spirit penetrating the cross of matter, uniting the two, showing how spirit descends into matter at birth or creation. Or it can be seen as the sun rising and sinking over the horizon, symbolizing the continuous cycle of birth and death, ie. eternal life.

The ankh appears on the top of Ptah's staff, the 'was' sceptre, which is the pictogram representing 'dominion'.

⊙   Ra, hru This symbol stands for the solar deities Ra and Heru (Horus), and also means 'day'. It is well-known today as the astrological symbol for the sun. The hieroglyph shows a dot which represents first beginnings, a seed, concentrated energy, a desire before it takes form as a thought. It is complete in itself, indivisible, the centre from which everything emanates and eventually returns.

The dot is surrounded by the circle of spirit, of timelessness, cyclic processes and completion. Therefore, like the creative solar deity Ra, the symbol denotes the beginning and the end, and the cycles of life which lie in between.

Khepera The symbol shows a dung beetle or scarab, a form in which the sun god Khepera is sometimes depicted. In nature the beetle lays its eggs in a ball of dung, which it then rolls along the ground, reminding the ancient Egyptians of the daily cycle of the sun's orb moving across the sky.

As a hieroglyph it is either used as a phonetic syllable or associated with the qualities of both the beetle and the god Khepera: to roll, to become, and to come into being.

Maat The feather is the symbol of the goddess of cosmic harmony, truth and justice, Maat, against which the heart of a deceased person was weighed in the Hall of Two Truths. It is also the hieroglyph for Shu, god of the atmosphere. Therefore, to the ancient Egyptians the hieroglyph would conjure up associations with these qualities, besides being a pictograph for a feather itself. In addition it can be used to write the syllables 'maat' or 'shu' within a word.

In a similar way words, by their very spelling, indicated their true nature.

This is shown in yet another creation story, that involving the solar god Ra of Heliopolis. Though he does not directly bring about materialization through words, nevertheless words play a part in the tale. The relationship between them is taken as a physical relationship between two things. When Ra wept, his tears, 'remy' in Egyptian, fell onto the earth from which man 'remet' sprang. His saliva 'netit' produced the gods 'neteru'.

Also using a play on words, the Egyptians believed that if a word was the reverse of another the meaning was also reversed. By this process the creator god Ptah's name reverses to 'htp', ie. hotep or hetep, meaning peace or offering. As an offering often involved the sacrifice of a living animal its life force was released from its body, its physical form, reversing the meaning of Ptah's name, 'force captured in form'.

All in a Name

Nor was Ptah's, or any other, name simply a name, but it held his essence, vibrated his nature. In a similar way numerologists today still believe that a person's name will affect their character and destiny, and that the sound vibration of a name can make for either a harmonious or a troubled life.

To the ancient Egyptians a name was a vital part of the self without which someone could not exist. Because of the power credited to the name an Egyptian was always given two, referred to as the 'true name' and the 'good name', or the 'great name' and the 'little name'. The 'good' or 'little' name was used openly in everyday life, but the 'true' or 'great' name was kept secret, as no harmful magic could be effective without the knowledge of an individual's real name.

Someone could curse an enemy or bless a friend by knowing his or her name. Sometimes pottery was inscribed with the name of an enemy and/or with a curse, and ritually broken as a way of destroying the actual person. A spell for overcoming the evil serpent Apep recommends making a wax image of the demon and writing his name on it. Then the image had to be burnt in a fire and the name destroyed with it, as simply destroying the figure was not sufficient. And, as the following story illustrates, if someone knew the true name of a god or a demon that being was compelled to do the magician's will.

The Story of Ra and Isis

The mighty sun god Ra ruled as king over both humans and gods. He was more ancient than time, so to him a hundred years were less than one year for mankind; and he possessed many magical names, unknown even to the gods.

Now Isis was only a mortal woman, though her magical skills exceeded those of other mortals and she possessed the words of power, given to her by Thoth. So great was her ambition that she aspired to rise above the mundane world of humankind and to become a goddess, equal to the mighty Ra himself. But to achieve this she needed to learn the secret name of the father of the gods. If she only knew his name she would have mastery over him and all his sacred knowledge.

Luckily for Isis, the creator god was so ancient that he dribbled at the mouth, and his spittle fell onto the earth. She took a handful of this and carefully kneeded it into the form of a poisonous serpent, which she brought to life by her words of power. She then placed it in Ra's path, at a spot where she knew he was sure to tread as he crossed his kingdom followed by his retinue of gods.

As Isis had planned, the serpent bit Ra and the poison seeped through his limbs causing him great pain, though he did not know what had caused it. He called out to the other gods in despair, asking for their help, saying, ' Let there be brought unto me my children, the gods, who possess the words of power and magical speech, and mouths which know how to utter them, and also powers which reach even unto the heavens.'

In answer to his summons all the gods hurried to him, filled with grief. Isis also came and calmly asked what ailed the king of the gods, 'Is it a serpent that hath bitten thee.......Verily it shall be cast down by my effective words of power, and I will drive it away from before the sight of thy sunbeams.'

When Ra agreed with her diagnosis, Isis continued with her plan, saying, 'O tell me thy name, holy Father, for whosoever shall be delivered by thy name shall live."

Ra, however, was as wily as Isis and hoped to be cured without divulging his secret name. Instead he tried to fool her by describing his many creations, and the names by which he was known at the different hours of the day. Meanwhile his pain increased and the poison continued to spread throughout his body.

But Isis was determined to know his true name before she would effect a cure and replied, ' What thou hast said is not thy name. O tell it unto me, and the poison shall depart.'

Though he was reluctant to give in, by this time Ra was suffering so much that he finally agreed to let Isis know his magical name. He hid away from the other gods, leaving the Boat of Millions of Years in which he travelled across the heavens, and divulged his most precious possession.

As soon as he had revealed the name to her Isis kept her oath and restored him to good health, and thereafter she possessed the power of the gods.

In Egyptian belief the name was included in the nine 'vehicles' that composed the entire person, physical and spiritual. These were: the 'khat' or physical body; the 'sahu', a form of spiritual body which was immortal and could live in the higher realms with the gods, and which contained the soul; the 'ka' or astral double; the 'ba' or soul; the 'ab' or heart, believed to be the seat of life and of good and evil; the 'khaibit', similar to the 'ka'; the 'khu' or spirit; and the 'sekhem' or power, believed to be the life spark.

The ninth vehicle was the name, 'ren' in Egyptian, which is written as shown. The letters r and n are followed by the determinative of a man with his hand touching his mouth, used to indicate things that are done with the mouth such as eating, or in this case speaking. It is interesting that the symbol for the first letter 'r' , representing an open mouth, links in with the determinative. It also shows how the sacred power of speech is shared with the name.

After death the preservation of a name was essential, or the spirit of the deceased would be destroyed. A person only came into being when his or her name was uttered, as at the beginning of time, therefore to be reborn in the afterlife, the Underworld gods had to know and speak the name. In the Hall of Two Truths a person who had no name could not be identified in order to be judged, and if proved 'true of voice' be permitted to join the gods.

An inscription in the pyramid of King Pepi I (c.2390-2361BC) states that Ra 'writeth down Pepi at the head of those who live.........Pepi goeth forward with his flesh, Pepi is happy with his name and he liveth with his ka.' And the pyramid of Pepi II contains a popular form of prayer for ensuring the survival of the name. This involves long lists of god names paired with the name of the deceased, for example, 'If the name of Ra flourisheth in the horizon, then the name of Pepi shall flourish.....'

In several historical cases a pharaoh has tried to obliterate all traces of a predecessor's name from his or her tomb, from statues and from other monumental inscriptions as a form of eternal punishment. This happened in the case of Hatshepsut (1473 - 1458 BC) who had usurped the throne of her nephew/step-son.

When Tuthmosis III finally became pharaoh in his own right he instructed masons to cut out her image and name from all monuments, condemning her to nothingness. He also removed her name from all lists of kings as if she had never existed.

The same fate befell Tutankhamen, his predecessor Akenaten and his successor Ay at the hands of General Horemheb, when he became pharaoh in 1319 BC. He erased the names of the royal Armanan family from all monuments, and on the king lists he wrote himself in as the successor of Amenophis III, Akenaten's father.

Though he did not destroy Tutankamen's tomb or take its treasure, Horemheb nevertheless abandoned the young king's soul to oblivion. His name had been erased from his statues and monuments and replaced with Horemheb's own. His tomb was forgotten, and he was deprived of the commemorative rites that would ensure eternal life. However, on one memorial statue at Karnak the king's name had been carved into the corner of the loincloth, hidden beneath gilded plaster and unnoticed by Horemheb's destructive stonemasons. So, according to Egyptian belief, despite Horemheb's worst efforts Tutankhamen's soul survived the millenia until his name was on the lips of millions in the twentieth century, ensuring his everlasting fame, if not everlasting life.

Texts that have come to be known as the 'Book of the Dead' were inscribed on the walls of tombs and sarcophagi, funeral stellae and papyri, with the intention of aiding the soul's rebirth in the Afterworld. These texts fulfilled a number of functions associated with the sacred powers of the word, and acted as a memory aid when the deceased was faced with reciting the formidable lists of names which were deemed essential for survival.

Firstly, the names of gods and demons dwelling in the halls of Duat had to be known in order to progress through them and to avoid being destroyed by evil entities. In the Hall of Two Truths the deceased was required to say, ' Homage to thee, O Great God, thou Lord of Maati...............I know thee, and I know thy name, and I know the names of the two and forty gods who exist with thee in this Hall of Maati."

Those who were judged worthy after having their heart weighed against the feather of Maat aquired the mystical name 'He who is equipped with the flowers and the dweller in his olive tree'. In order to progress further on the demanding Underworld journey this 'password' then had to be spoken.

It was also essential for the deceased to name all the parts of the Hall of Maati, such as doors, posts, bolts, lintels and the floor itself. Furthermore,the name of the Guardian of the Hall and the name of Osiris, Lord of Duat, had to be recalled before the deceased's own name could be presented to the latter.

In the Underworld it was necessary to pass through seven halls, and at each gate to know the names of the doorkeeper, the watcher and the herald who guarded them. If it safely negotiated these the soul then faced twenty one pylons which again had to be named, along with the doorkeeper of each.

To travel in the Field of Reeds, the Egyptian heaven, the soul needed a boat in order to cross its many streams. Therefore, a boat was drawn on papyrus along with the relevant chapters from the 'Book of the Dead' and placed in the tomb. If the deceased could recite these chapters correctly the image of the boat would become an actual boat. Though, naturally, before the deceased could climb aboard each part of the boat had to be told its magical name. Even after he or she had mastered these names, the deceased then had to recite the true name of the river, its banks and the ground. And finally, on gaining free access to the Field of Reeds, the deceased still had to guard against the snares and nets set by evil entities which lived there. The only way to escape the 'fishers' was to know the correct names of their nets, and for each part of the net such as the ropes, the poles and the hooks.

From these involved procedures it can be seen that knowledge of hundreds of names, and the right vibration of them, was a prerequisite for survival in the afterlife. The name gave life, and the preservation of a person's own name and the recital of other names maintained it for eternity.

WoRds of Power

A similar idea to that shown in the 'Book of the Dead' spell for making a picture of a boat transform into a real boat existed in relation to food, drink and all the other necessities for survival in Duat. It was thought that the recitation of the appropriate words of power, known in ancient Egyptian as 'hekau', could bring images and pictures to life, creating tasty food and thirst-quenching drink. The correct words and prayers could also preserve the mummified body from corruption for all eternity.

Reciting magical passages from the 'Book of the Dead' gave the deceased the use of his or her body and faculties in the next world. The heart was of prime importance here as it was regarded as the seat of life, and one text was even designed to animate a heart amulet, thus providing the deceased with a 'new' heart. This was necessary as the physical heart had been removed during the mummification process and was preserved separately from the body.

The heart amulet was usually in the form of a scarab symbolizing Khepera, the creator and sustainer of life. The text begins: 'May my heart be with me in the House of Hearts! May my breast be with me in the House of Hearts!..........' It was then vital to recite further chapters in order to prevent the physical heart from being carried away by a demon which had a penchant for stealing them.

Magical words placed with the dead were considered so important that a text in the pyramid of Unas states: 'The bone and flesh which possess no writing are wretched....'

In life, as well as in death, knowledge of the 'hekau' was invaluable. It was believed that a priest or magician vibrating these words in the correct way could heal, perform exorcisms or shape-shift. Even the elements could be commanded to obey the magician's will if the correct words were uttered.

All beings, divine, demonic or mortal could not stand against the might of the 'hekau'. During the 'opening of the mouth' ceremony, when the deceased was given the words of power which would be needed for survival in the Underworld, he or she was also given the ability to vibrate them correctly, so that gods and other entities would listen and obey.

As shown in her encounter with Ra, the goddess Isis was mistress of the words of power. During her travels with her son Horus, after his father Osiris was murdered by Set, they were accomp-anied by seven scorpions. When one of these stung the governor's son in the land where she was staying Isis said, 'Come to me, come to me. For my word is a talisman which beareth life. I am a daughter well known in thy city also, and I will do away the evil by means of the word of my mouth.'

Whilst laying healing hands on the boy Isis continued chanting, 'I am Isis, the goddess, the lady of words of power, who doeth deeds of magic, the words of whose voice are charms.' Then, by uttering further magical words, she restored the child to full health. Though the words of power could create, heal and preserve there are also many ancient Egyptian accounts of magicians complete-ly destroying an enemy by reciting a few correct words accomp-anied by a simple ritual.

A short story from the Ptolemaic period illustrates the Egyptian reverence for magical words, and the lengths that some people were willing to go to in order to master the secrets:

The Tale of Setnau

The Prince Setnau was a master of magic and the possessor of words of power. However, he was always seeking to improve his arcane knowledge and to this end he set out one day along with his brother Anhaherurau in search of the tomb of Ptah-nefer-ka in Memphis, which was reputed to contain a sacred book written by the god Thoth himself. In this book, it was said, were two formulae, the first bestowing power over all heaven and earth, the second enabling a dead man to assume the form he had while living.

After three days and three nights of searching the brothers finally found the tomb, where Setnau recited a spell to make the ground open up. As the two men descended into the hollow beneath the sepulchre they were surprised to find it brightly lit - the source of the light none other than the sacred book. They also found the living doubles of the magician Ptah-nefer-ka, his wife Ahura and their son Merhu in occupation of the tomb.

When Setnau told Ahura of his intentions she begged him not to take the book, claiming that misfortune attended the possessor of it, as the case of Ptah-nefer-ka proved.

Her husband had learnt of the writings through a priest of Ptah, who in return for a reward disclosed that they could be found in an iron box in the middle of the Nile at Coptos. Ptah-nefer-ka in turn told the pharaoh about the book, and after some days had passed he and his family set sail for Coptos in the royal barge.

Using his words of power Ptah-nefer-ka turned a model raft into the real thing and images of workmen equipped with tools into living men. The search then began. It continued for three days and three nights before the box was finally found and the serpents and scorpions within it dispersed by further incantations.

Ptah-nefer-ka was filled with anticipation as he took the book back to the royal barge, nor was he disappointed. When he read the first of the two formulae it contained he learnt all the secrets of the heavens and the earth, and when he read the second he saw the sun god rise in the heavens with his glorious retinue of gods. Ahura also read the sacred writings and experienced the same visions as her husband had done.

Wishing to absorb the power of the book Ptah-nefer-ka copied its contents onto a piece of papyrus, which he dissolved in water and drank, giving him awesome knowledge. However, his action displeased Thoth, who reported the matter to Ra.

All Ptah-nefer-ka's new-found power was not sufficient to protect him and his family against the wrath of the gods, and the three of them were punished by drowning in the river as they returned home with the book.

Despite its tragic ending Ahura's tale failed to deter Setnau from his objective and he agreed to play draughts against Ptah-nefer-ka for possession of his book. When Setnau triumphed, even in the face of Ptah-nefer-ka's attempts at cheating, he immediately sent Anhaherurau up to collect his talismans of Ptah and the magical papyri which had been left outside the tomb.

As soon as the talismans were placed on him Setnau ascended to the realms of the gods, clasping the sacred book and surrounded by a halo of light, his dream finally fulfilled.

Ptah-nefer-ka, on the other hand, was not pleased to see his prize possession go in this way and vowed that one day it would be returned. And eventually, after Setnau had experienced many adventures, the book was indeed brought back to the tomb, on the pharaoh's orders.

Creative Words Pathworking

Mythologically, in the story of Ptah the power of the word, combined with inspiration and willpower, brought about the first creation. But also in a modern context this combination presents opportunities for 'creation', for making new opportunities, for bringing into manifestation what is vital and positive. The myth is so valuable because it offers eternal, ongoing possibilities, and partaking in it awakens our own creative potential.

If you are unfamiliar with the term, a pathworking is a form of active meditation or visualization, designed to increase awareness of a subject, and to help effect changes in everyday life. Through the following pathworking you can personally experience the power of the creative word, but only perform it when you are in a condition to make the most of its benefits, not when you are over-tired, depressed or unduly preoccupied.

Before starting make sure that you will not be disturbed by anyone and that the 'phone is off the hook. Then sit comfortably, close your eyes, and breathe slowly and regularly for a while until you feel relaxed.

You sink deeper into meditation until you find yourself in a warm and peaceful ocean where nothing exists except your own consciousness. There is no substance, no time and no direction, only your consciousness. You find it perfectly easy to breathe underwater. All is calm and safe, and you rest for a while.

Then you begin to contemplate your being. Who are you? At present you have no physical substance, but you can formulate a thought. That thought is your only identity. As your thoughts develop and the identity becomes clearer it centres on a name, your name. Whisper it aloud. Then speak it louder and louder, gaining strength and confidence each time. The name has power, your own power and faith in yourself.

Now you have established your identity. You truly exist. When you feel ready meditate on your name and how it relates to everything you feel about this identity. Be aware that you are at the centre of your own inner universe and are at peace there.

Then, after a little time you begin to feel a sense of dissatisfaction. Something is lacking, but it is in your power to bring about change. You need more than peace and darkness.

You need a sense of stability, firm ground, direction. Think of the earth, its quality, texture, what it means to you. Then you speak the word 'earth', and find that you are standing on solid ground. Feel it beneath your feet and experience a sense of security.

But though it is safe, the water now seems too restrictive. You want to experience something new, another element. You think of the freedom of air, the clarity and freshness, and any other thoughts that come to you. Softly you speak the word 'air'. As you do so slowly the earth on which you are standing begins to rise above the waters, forming a dome-shaped island. For the first

43

time you feel the touch of the wind on your face. You fill your lungs with fresh air, breathing deeply, enjoying the new sensation. You feel a sense of freedom, but still something is lacking.

Light. Think about all it means. Then say the word and watch the sun rise for the first time in the east. Now you can identify direction. And by the sun's illumination you can see the shimmering ocean and the solid land. You are moved by the beauty around you, but you also know that it is your creation. Its source is within you. Everything can be found within, though it requires deep thought, understanding and will-power to manifest it.

Though you are surrounded by the four elements, water, air, earth and fire, in the form of the sun, you are still the only living being in your inner universe. The earth is bare, with no plants or trees, the sea has no fish, and there are no animals or humans.

Think of and speak all that you wish to create. Perhaps some things, such as snakes, spiders, volcanos, etc, will come to mind though initially you do not want to create them. Not everything in your inner universe is going to be idyllic, or it would not be balanced, but remember that they are all a part of you and therefore under your control. It is quite safe to face them, rather than trying to ignore what is negative.

You do not necessarily have to think and name things that are visible, but qualities such as compassion. Your own imagination is your limit. What do you feel is particularly needed in your life at the moment?

In your inner universe you can create it. Savour the sense of joy and strength, knowing that you have the power to make positive changes, to make your dreams come true.

When you feel you have reached a stage when you are satisfied with your achievement, slowly return to normal consciousness, keeping your eyes shut for a couple of minutes. Then look around at your physical surroundings, taking them in to make sure you are properly 'earthed'. Finally, have a hot drink or something to eat to complete the 'earthing' process.

This pathworking or a similar one of your own devising can then be performed as many times as you feel is helpful.

Chapter Three

In the Beginning.......

The ancient Egyptians called their hieroglyphs the 'words of the god', though they never had one sacred book in which all doctrine was written down. Instead it was found in numerous inscriptions and papyri. The Hebrews also believed that their god gave sacred words to mankind, including both the alphabet and laws for religious practice and correct living. Originally the revelations believed to have been directly received from the Hebrew god were written down on many separate documents, which were later compiled into one volume. Together with the early history of the Hebrew people, it is now collectively known as the Old Testament, thought to literally contain the divine word. Nor is this belief relegated to history and the past, but one still subscribed to by many Jews and Christians.

Throughout their varied and turbulent history the ancient Hebrews came into close contact with many other Middle Eastern peoples of their time, either through trade or from living as captives. As a result Hebrew religious beliefs have much in common with those of neighbouring cultures, beliefs such as their creation myth, which bears a close resemblence to the Egyptian version involving Ptah, Thoth or Khepera, and also to Sumerian and Babylonian tales.

Historical Background

Sumeria and Babylonia
The Sumerians inhabited land near the Persian Gulf, south of Babylonia which centered on the Tigris and Euphrates rivers. To

the north of Babylonia, still based around these two rivers, was the kingdom of Assyria and to the west, the land of the Hebrews.

The Sumerians are thought to have arrived in southern Mesopotamia around 4000 BC, by which time they had already developed a reasonably advanced culture. They were a non-Semetic race whose original homeland is not known for certain, though different authorities suggest the Iranian highlands, central Asia, or the Indus Valley. The new-comers mingled with the existing population of the area, adopting their lifestyle but supplanting the native tongue with Sumerian.

Gradually the small agricultural communities grew larger, as sophisticated irrigation techniques were developed, until eventually they united to form city-states such as Ur. These flourished from around 4000 - 2000 BC, with each state centred around the temple. The role of High Priest and king was filled by one individual belonging to a ruling dynasty, who, like the Egyptian pharaoh, was regarded as divine.

The Sumerians were an inventive and advanced people, who formulated their own system of writing, the earliest deciphered example of which dates to around 3000 BC.

To the north of the Sumerian lands lay those of a Semetic people, probably originating from northern Syria, who are referred to as Babylonians after their main city, and whose language was Akkadian, which came to be the earliest written Semetic language. At first they lived peacefully with their southern neighbours, accepting their supremacy, until around 1762 BC when the Babylonian king Hammurabi united the two kingdoms by a series of political and military coups. The conquering Babylonians adopted Sumerian mythology and literature, translating it into Akkadian, with the result that the two belief systems fused into one.

The first dynasty of Babylon fell in 1595 BC, after which the kingdom was occupied by a series of invaders from neighbouring lands. Then, in 745 BC Babylonia was conquered by the

5. Primitive Sumerian pictograms on a limestone tablet from
Kish, c.3500 BC

Assyrian, Tiglath Pileser III, who was followed by his son, Shalmaneser IV.

In the sixth century BC the Chaldean, Nebuchadnezzar II, instigated many technical advances during his long reign. However, following his death in 562 BC civil war erupted, and order was not restored until 555 BC when Nabonidus became king, ruling until the Persian conquest of Babylon under Cyrus in 539 BC.

The Hebrews
Entwined with the fate of the Assyrio-Babylonian empire is the early history of the Hebrew people, which will be familiar to readers of the Old Testament. And, though it has a strong mythological element, the historical side of the account is based on actual events.

Since the sixth century BC members of the tribe of Judah, their legendary patriarch and ancestor, were known as Jews, though the name is also applied to the tribe descended from Abraham, who was said to have come from Mesopotamia to Canaan around 2000 BC.

According to the Old Testament, when famine hit Canaan Abraham's grandson Israel (or Jacob) was invited by his son Joseph to go to Egypt, where the latter was chief minister to the pharaoh. Due to his rank Joseph obtained permission for the Hebrews to settle the land of Goshen, where they lived in peace and prosperity for several generations, becoming aquainted with Egyptian beliefs. However, when a new dynasty took the throne of Egypt the settlers were deprived of all their former rights and found themselves reduced to slavery.

They remained in this position until the latter half of the second millenium BC when a suitable leader emerged, a man who possessed the right skills to deliver them to freedom. Moses, the leader of the Exodus, was an Egyptian-trained magician and master of the words of power, as stated in Acts vii. 22: he 'was mighty in words and deeds'. These powers enabled him and his people to escape the Egyptian pharaoh, probably Ramesses II, by inflicting plagues on the Egyptians at the command of the Hebrew god.

Three months after Moses had led his people out of Egypt his god spoke directly to him on Mount Sinai, giving him a Written Law which was known as the *Torah she-bi-khetav*. On the same occasion he was given the Oral Law or *Torah she-be-al-peh*, which consisted of interpretations of the Written Law.

"And the Lord said unto Moses, Come up to me into the mount, and be there: and I will give thee tables of stone, and a law, and commandments which I have written; that thou mayest teach them."

"............And Moses turned, and went down from the Mount, and the two tables of the testimony were in his hand: the tables were written on both their sides; on the one side and on the other were they written. And the tables were the work of God, and the writing was the writing of God, graven upon the tables."

Moses' successor Joshua led the Hebrews on to Canaan, the 'land of promise' - which today includes Syria, Lebanon, Jordan and Israel - conquering and driving out the existing inhabitants. When they reached the city of Jericho his god commanded Joshua to arrange for seven ram's horn trumpets to be sounded and for the people to shout simultaneously. This combined effort, illustrating the power of sound vibration, caused the massive walls to crumble, enabling Joshua to take the city.

The land around the Jordan was then divided amongst the Hebrew tribes, but due to a lack of unity between these tribes they were often subdued by peoples from the surrounding lands. Eventually, in order to establish cohesion, Saul was chosen as king around 1033 BC, in place of the the previous system of republican chiefs.

During the reign of Solomon (c.970-933), which saw a major

flourishing of culture, a temple was built in Jerusalem and the Hebrews established trade with many peoples. These included the Phoenicians, whose alphabetic characters are the basis for the Hebrew letters.

After Solomon's death dissension led to the division of the Hebrews into two kingdoms: Judah under Rehoboam, Solomon's son, and Israel under Jeroboam, from the tribe of Ephraim. The kingdom of Judah was made up of the tribes of Judah and Benjamin, while Israel comprised the remaining ten tribes.

Around two hundred years later the kingdom of Israel was conquered by Shalmaneser IV and Sargon II of Assyria, and in 721 BC most of the Israelite people were sent to Media as captives. The kingdom of Judah survived longer, but in 586 BC its capital, Jerusalem, fell to Nebuchadnezzar II, who burnt the temple and sent the most powerful and wealthy citizens in captivity to Babylon. It was during this period that the Mosaic Laws were strongy enforced and most of the Oral Law evolved.

After he had been declared king of Babylon in 539 BC, the Persian Cyrus allowed foreign captives, including the Jews, to return to their native lands, though many chose to remain in Mesopotamia. Those who did return to Jerusalem arranged for work to begin on a new temple to replace the one which had been destroyed, and this was completed in 516 BC. Later, during the reign of another Persian, Artaxerxes, the Jews enforced the strict observance of the Written Law, and their sacred records began to be compiled and transcribed.

Language anò Letters

Cuneiform
The oldest of the ancient Middle Eastern scripts is cuneiform, meaning wedge-shaped, which was invented by the ancient Sumerians at the end of the fourth millenium BC, and later adopted by the Babylonians for their inscriptions and documents. As is the case with other alphabets, its characters originated as

pictographs, which in time evolved into angular letters, written from left to right. Like the pictographs, these were inscribed with a stylus on clay tablets, then baked or sun-dried to preserve them.

Because the Babylonian or Akkadian language differed from Sumerian some changes were needed to accomodate consonants which did not exist in the latter tongue, though the Babylonians borrowed many words from Sumeria. The most famous document written in Akkadian cuneiform, in this case engraved on stone, was the law code of King Hammurabi (c.1792-1750 BC). Sumerian/ Babylonian myths such as the 'Epic of Creation' and the 'Epic of Gilgamesh' were also inscribed in cuneiform around the same period, after being transmitted orally for generations.

The Assyrians spoke a different dialect to the Babylonians, but they too used the cuneiform script, which is found on their royal inscriptions and administrative letters. During the period of Assyrian domination in the Middle East Akkadian was gradually replaced by Aramaic, which was written alphabetically on parchment. Cuneiform finally ceased to be used shortly before the Christian era, and was not deciphered until the middle of the nineteenth century by a man named Henry Rawlinson.

Hebrew
In contrast to the other languages and scripts of the ancient Middle East, which are long since extinct, Hebrew still survives in its modern form. In addition, it is found in biblical or classical and post-biblical or rabbinic forms.

The language is of the north western branch of the Semetic group, to which Phoenician also belongs, and it was from the Phoenician script, developed around the end of the second millenium BC, that the Hebrew characters evolved. Though Hebrew letters no longer bear any real resemblance to actual objects, they began as pictographic representations, and have always been written from right to left.

Sumerian	Ideogram	Semetic	Meaning
ad		abu	father
gir		kîru	smelting furnace
udun		utûnu	oven, stove
gu		alpu	horned cattle
ama		rîmu	wild steer
ulu		ullu	splendour
ulu		ulßu	shout with joy
du		asâmu	to be fitting

The above example of Assyrian cuneiform, dating from the 7th Century BC, is taken from one of a number of clay tablets found at Kuyunjik (Nineveh). It is in effect a dictionary, giving the Sumerian name of each word with its Semetic translation, and would have been used as a teaching aid at a time when syllabic and ideogrammatic scripts were being converted to alphabetic ones.

Assyrian Cuneiform

Originally Hebrew had only 22 consonants and no written vowels, though u and i came to be represented by the consonants vau and yod respectively. Later, in the early Christian era, a group of Hebrew scribes devised a system of vowels, written above or beneath the neighbouring consonant.

A central aspect of the Jewish esoteric philosophy known as the Qabalah, described below, is the sanctity of the Hebrew alphabet, arising from a belief that the letters were vibrated at the moment of creation and that they also play an integral part in the continuation of life. Linked to this concept, the letters are used as the basis for a system of correspondences and numerology, which give an understanding of the interaction between all things in creation and how to work in harmony with them.

Gods of the Creative Word

Yaweh - The Logos
The god of the Bible not only spoke the creative word, but he was that word, as the Gospel According to St John says, 'In the beginning was the Word, and the Word was with God, and the Word was God.'

In Genesis: '*God said, let there be light: and there was light.........And God called the light Day...........God said let there be a firmament in the midst of the waters, and let it divide the waters from the waters..........And God called the firmament Heaven.....*' By this means all creation came into being at the creator's word, and not only did he bring everything into being through his word, he also named each thing. As in the beliefs of many other cultures, here the naming of a thing was important in giving it true existence.

The biblical god spoke the word in order to bring about creation, from his own consciousness he created a universe, a reflection of himself, which enabled him to achieve full self-realization. This has a parallel in the fact that humans can only appreciate past and future, or be properly conscious of the self once we have language, either as a race through evolution, or individually when we learn to speak. When we utter our first word, in a sense that marks the beginning of our personal universe, one which we can name and analyse.

The sacred name of the biblical god, JHVH, the primal creative word itself, is known by the Greek word Tetragrammaton, referring to the four letters in its Hebrew spelling. These derive from the passage in Exodus when his god instructs Moses to lead the Jewish people from captivity in Egypt.

Moses asks, "*Behold, when I come unto the children of Israel, and shall say unto them, the God of your fathers has sent me unto you; and they shall say to me, What is his name? what shall I say unto them?*

'*And God said unto Moses, "I AM THAT I AM: and he said, Thus shalt thou say unto the children of Israel, I AM hath sent me unto you."*'

In biblical Hebrew the verb 'to be' also means 'to breathe', associated with life and creation and with speech. Genesis 2 states that: 'The Lord God formed man of the dust of the ground, and breathed into his nostrils the breath of life; and man became a living soul.'

Because the Hebrew god was the creative word, the correct pronunciation of JHVH was thought to contain awesome power. For this reason it was never spoken aloud except under exceptional circumstances, and he was instead referred to by other titles or by the Tetragrammaton. The true pronunciation of the name has been lost and cannot be deduced with certainty, as ancient Hebrew was written without vowels. It is said that the divine being himself withdrew his true name from a fallen people because it holds too great a power for us to handle. The closest approximation we have is Yaweh or Jehovah, by which names the Old Testament god is usually known.

Tradition claims that Moses vibrated the name of his god to part the Red Sea, and that each year the High Priest at the Temple of Jerusalem pronounced it in the Holy of Holies. But on the tongue of any but the highest adept it could prove dangerous. 'He who can rightly pronounce it, causeth heaven and earth to tremble, for it is the name which rusheth through the universe.'

It was believed that pronouncing Yaweh's name correctly would give direct realization of the divine presence, causing the person invoking it to be shattered by his lightning descent: 'For no man may look upon the face of God and live.'

Besides JHVH, there are three less well-known Hebrew names for their god: ADNI, meaning 'Lord', and pronounded Adonai by western Qabalists; AHIH, said 'eieie', meaning pure existence or 'I am'; and AGLA, comprising the initial letters for the phrase 'thou art mighty for ever O Lord' written in Hebrew, and representing unity. These latter three are part of the seventy-two syllabled divine name or the Shemahamphorash. Just as the Egyptian Ra was described as having numerous secret and powerful names which could be used to produce effects, the god of the Hebrews also possessed many names, comprising the Shemahamphorash.

According to tradition, the pronunciation of this was lost from ancient times until around 300 AD when Qabalists re-discovered it and reduced its many syllables to JHVH. They accomplished this by using a variation of Gematria (see below) in which the numerical values of the letters JHVH were added in an alternative way to produce seventy two, ie. equal to the component names of the Shemahamphorash, rather than the usual gematric number of the Tetragrammaton which is twenty six.

Yaweh's true name was believed by Qabalists to be concealed in the words of the sacred scriptures, and some even believed that the entire Torah comprised the holy name.

Enlil - Creator and Destroyer

Parallels can be seen between the biblical creator and Enlil, ancient Sumerian god of storm and air, who was believed to utter the words of power which had control over all creation.

According to myth, Nammu, the goddess personifying the primordial waters of chaos, gave birth to the first being, An-Ki, or heaven and earth, who in turn gave birth to Enlil.

However, as they were still one at this time, Enlil had to separate them in order for the creation process to continue. He then took his mother Ki, or earth, as his wife, and together they produced the other gods and all life on earth: human, animal and plant. In this way Enlil personifies the breath or active word of his father An, the god of heaven:

'Your word - it is plants, your word - it is grain,

Your word is the floodwater, the life of all the lands.'

While An remains in a higher dimension, further removed from mankind, Enlil acts as his agent. But, just as Enlil's words could be creative, they also had the power to wreak devastation:

'The word of Enlil is a breath of wind, the eye sees it not.

'His word is a deluge which advances and has no rival.

His word above the slumbering skies makes the earth to slumber.

His word when it comes in humility destroys the country.

His word when it comes in majesty overwhelms houses and brings weeping to the land.

At his word the heavens on high are stilled.'

6. Adad, the Assyrian counterpart of Enlil, depicted as a storm-god armed with thunderbolts. Based on a relief from Arslan-Tash, c. Eighth century BC.

Another of Enlil's roles was as the maker of earthly kings. So powerful was his word that simply by speaking the name of the man he had chosen to rule the god raised him above the rest of humankind, enabling him to fulfil his destiny.

Like the god of the Hebrews, Enlil appeared in the power of the storm, and also like Yaweh, he sent a deluge in order to punish mankind by annihilation.

The Babylonians, who adopted the Sumerian deities, assimilated him to their chief god Marduk, also known as Bel, meaning Lord. In Assyria he was identified with the god Adad, who presided over both destructive tempests and life-giving rain.

The Qabalah and Jewish Mysticism

The Qabalah - also spelt Qabbala, Cabbala, Kabbala and Kabala - is an ancient system believed to have been received by the patriarch Abraham. It is, however, not accepted by exoteric Judaism, and the two belief systems vary in certain vital aspects.

The name, QBL in Hebrew, literally means 'from mouth to ear', showing that it was largely an oral tradition, passed down from initiate to pupil and kept secret from the profane who might misuse the teachings.

Nevertheless, the doctrine was set down in written form: firstly in the *Sepher Yetzirah*, or *Book of Formation*, which dates from the second century AD; secondly in the *Zohar*, or *Book of Splendour*, published in the sixteenth century. Though critics claim that the latter was actually written by the Spanish Rabbi Moses de Leon in the late thirteenth century, it is more likely that he compiled and edited a number of earlier manuscripts, rather than composing the book himself.

In the Garden of Eden, besides the Tree of Knowledge from which Adam and Eve ate, there was also the Tree of Life, uniting the earth and the heavens, both trees symbolic of metaphysical conditions. The Tree of Life, as pictorially represented, consists

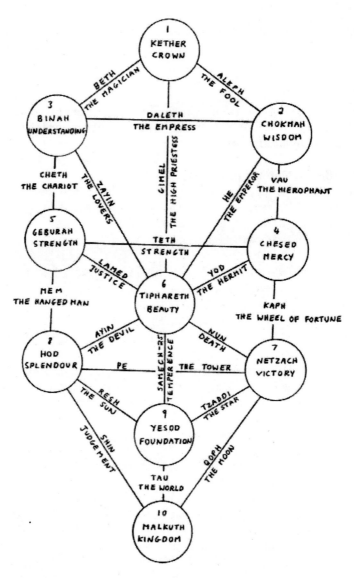

The Tree of Life - Giving the Tarot card attributions for the paths.

of a diagram depicting all creation, offering a way of understanding and working with what lies beyond intellectual comprehension.

A major difference between Qabalism and exoteric Judaism is the Qabalistic doctrine that the god of Genesis is only an emanation of a 'higher' transcendent deity described as three veils of negative existence: 'Ain' meaning 'negativity', 'Ain Soph', meaning 'the limitless' or 'without end', and 'Ain Soph Aour' or 'absolute limitless light'. This unbeing being, who was and yet was not, 'existed' in the very beginning, preceding the god responsible for creation. The latter manifested in a series of emanations known as the sephiroth, represented on the Tree as spheres, finally bringing the material world into existence. At each level the essence of the divine became less spiritual, and more dense, as it descended into matter.

The highest, most refined, sephira is Kether, the Crown, symbolizing the creative godhead. This godhead had a thought, like Ptah in Egyptian mythology, and the thought divided into two, represented by the second and third sephiroth, Chokmah and Binah. Chokmah, at the head of the right or 'male' side of the Tree, also referred to as the right hand pillar, is entitled Wisdom and symbolizes the primal masculine energy. Binah, Understanding, at the head of the left or 'female' side of the Tree, or left hand pillar, represents the cosmic mother, receptive where Chokmah is active.

At the next level of manifestation the sephira Chesed, Justice, occupies a place directly below Chokmah, and represents mercy, order and protection, the qualities of a loving father; while Geburah, or Severity, on the left side of the Tree, stands for the notion of the dark goddess who destroys what is outworn in order to make way for the new. Below them, forming an inverted triangle, is Tiphareth, or Beauty, the centre of equilibrium of the Tree. It symbolizes balance and harmony, redemption and transformation, lying on the middle pillar beneath Kether, pure spirit, and above Malkuth, the realm of the four elements.

On a lower level again are Netzach on the right, Hod on the left. The former has the title of Victory and is associated with the instincts, emotions, elemental energy and the forces of nature. Hod, or Glory, on the left, symbolizes the intellectual faculties and the rational mind, therefore governing magic and the power of the will.

Finally, on the middle pillar lie Yesod and Malkuth. Yesod, bearing the title of Foundation, relates to the astral plane, dreams, psychism and imagination, while Malkuth is the most material sephira, the sphere of the elements and of manifestation, known as the Kingdom.

The same principle of divine descent into matter, seen symbolically as a lightning flash connecting all ten sephiroth, is also thought to be true of the human spirit. Though Qabalists believe that it is possible for a person to regain this lost divinity through the practice of mysticism, the ascent being represented by the serpent of wisdom with its head in Kether. In Qabalistic tradition the universe, or Macrocosm, exists in identical form in man, the Microcosm, and the paths and spheres are symbolically present in each human being.

The ten sephiroth are also associated with the letters of the divine name or Tetragrammaton, which permeates all things. Yod, He, Vau and He correspond to nine of the sephiroth on the Tree of Life: Yod to Chokmah (Wisdom), the creative energy; He to Binah (Understanding), the primal mother; Vau to the six spheres from Chesed to Yesod; and the final He to Malkuth (the Kingdom), the world of manifestation. Therefore, according to the Qabalists, the name and life-spirit (breath) of the creator exists on all planes of creation and within all things.

Correspondences are also made between the four letters of the Tetragrammaton and the Four Worlds of the Qabalists, the four elements of the alchemists, the division of the Zodiac into triplicities, ie. cardinal, mutable and fixed, with four signs in each, and the four Tarot suits:

Yod	He	Vau	He
Atziluth	Briah	Yetzirah	Assiah
Fire	Water	Air	Earth
Wands	Cups	Swords	Pentacles

Some aspects of Medieval and modern Qabalism, such as the above associations with the Tarot and with alchemical lore, do not derive from the early Hebrew writings, but as a living system the Qabalah is forever changing, and not only the most ancient roots are valid.

Correspondences of the Hebrew Alphabet

As Yaweh's own name is his life-giving breath or creative word, the twenty two Hebrew letters and their corresponding paths joining the sephiroth on the Tree of Life are also its manifestations. They represent an integral part of his creation, in which all things are linked and can affect each other.

The *Sepher Yetzirah* says:

'Ten are the ineffable sephiroth, twenty two are the letters; the foundation of all things.....Ten is the number of the voices from the void, and unto them are ten regions of infinity, infinite in beginning and infinite in ending; infinite in goodness and infinite in evil; infinite in height and infinite in depth; infinite to the east and infinite to the west; infinite to the north and infinite to the south......The ten sephiroth appear as a flash of lightning from out of the infinite void; the word (logos) is in them as they emanate and as they return......The voices from the void project ten numbers: first is spirit, the spirit of the living god......Second, from the spirit is produced air, and within air are shaped the twenty-two sounds, the holy letters of the alphabet. Third, from the air is shaped the waters, and from formlessness emerges mud

The Hebrew Alphabet - Giving the numerical values for the letters

and clay of earth. Fourth, from the water is created fire, and a throne of fire as the seat of the highest.....'

Each letter of the Hebrew alphabet has a name, the initial letter of which is used in writing. Each also possesses an individual meaning, deriving from the pictograph which originally represented that letter.

There are numerous correspondences attached to the letters: animals, incense, precious stones, plants and metals, to name but a few. I have not placed these under the letter meanings, but full listings can be found in Aleister Crowley's '777'. Please refer to the bibliography for details.

Aleph Numerical value - 1
Aleph is referred to as one of the three 'mothers' of the Hebrew alphabet, representing the elements which were believed to be the basis of all creation. Aleph is linked with the element of air, joining the earth and heaven. Relating to this is the correspondence in man the microcosm with the chest, containing the lungs and therefore associated with air and breath.

With the numerical value of one, Aleph represents unity. Its meaning is cattle or ox, the letter shape originally depicting either a yoke, a ploughshare or the horned head of a bull. It can be interpreted as wealth, the origin of this association being the prime importance of cattle in a pastoral society, where a man's status was measured by the number in his herd, and where human welfare depended on cattle.

As the initial letter of the alphabet Aleph also represents the person of first importance in a household, namely the father, in the patriarchal tradition of the ancient Hebrews.

On the wheel of the year Aleph corresponds to spring and autumn, the seasons of the equinoxes. Its Tarot correspondence is the Fool.

Beth Numerical value - 2

Beth is one of the seven 'doubles' of the Hebrew alphabet, which rank second in importance after the three 'mothers', its dual nature relating to life and death. According to the Sepher Yetzirah the seven planets known in ancient times and the seven days of the week had their origin in the 'doubles', Beth's planetary correspondence being Mercury.

The meaning of Beth is a house, from which the letter shape derives, probably depicting the roof, floor and one wall. Therefore, this character is associated with safety and stability. It also has associations with the family, ancestors and descendants, and the foundation of the family centred around the ancestral home.

As the first letter of Genesis, Beth represents divine creation, which on the mundane plane relates to human pro-creation. As Aleph is the letter of the father, Beth corresponds to the mother.

The 'doubles' relate to the seven directions of Hebrew tradition, which consist of north, south, east, west, above, below and centre. Beth's direction is above and its Tarot correspondence is the Magician.

Gimel Numerical value - 3

This letter is the second of the 'doubles', relating to the Moon and to the opposite qualities of harmony and conflict. It has the meaning of camel, from which its interpretation is drawn. Just as the camel is able to survive in desert conditions through its capacity to store water and nutrients, Gimel represents strength of character, the ability to face difficulties on all levels and to come through them satisfactorily.

Gimel corresponds to the direction below and to the Tarot card of the High Priestess.

Daleth Numerical value - 4

As the third 'double', Daleth has the dual nature of knowledge and ignorance, and the planetary attribution of Venus. Its symbolic meaning is a door, indicated by the letter shape which resembles a porch. Daleth is therefore a gateway to progress for some, while for others it is a closed door, hindering or stopping them from advancing either spiritually or materially.

The cardinal point relating to Daleth is the east, and in the Tarot pack it is associated with the Empress.

He Numerical value - 5

He is the first of the letters referred to as 'simple', of which there are twelve, corresponding to the signs of the zodiac and to certain human faculties. In the case of He, this is the sense of sight and the sign of Aries, the ram.

The letter has the meaning of a window, shown by the space between the two strokes of the character shape. Through a window light and air are able to reach those inside a building, therefore, He symbolically links the inner with the outer on all levels, and is associated with mystical illumination. He is both the second and the final letter of the Tetragrammaton, the first giving of form by the Great Mother Binah, and the final manifestation of Malkuth. In the Tarot He corresponds to the Emperor, or according to some sources to the Star.

Vau (V and U) Numerical Value - 6

Vau is the second of the simple letters, linked with the sign of Taurus and the faculty of hearing. Pictorially and symbolically it indicates a nail. This can be seen as a fixed axis, around which the stars and planets revolve, giving it an association with time.

Vau is the third letter of the Tetragrammaton, relating to all the Sephiroth from Chesed to Yesod. Its Tarot correspondence is the Hierophant.

Zayin Numerical value - 7

As the third 'simple' letter, Zayin is associated with Gemini and with the sense of smell. The meaning and shape of this letter represents a sword, with the upper Yod depicting the hilt above the blade. However, it does not denote aggression, as the sword is seen as sheathed. Rather, it symbolizes rest and peace backed up by power. Zayin's Tarot attribution is the Lovers.

Cheth Phonetic Value - Ch. Numerical value - 8

Cheth, the third 'simple' letter, relates to the zodiac sign of Cancer and to the faculty of speech. Its meaning is a fence, and as such it represents a barrier or division, separating the inner from the outer. Therefore, this letter stands for choice and discrimination. In the Tarot its correspondence is the Chariot.

Teth Numerical value - 9

The 'simple' letter Teth relates to Leo, and to the sense of taste. Its meaning is a serpent, as is shown by the letter shape. The astrological symbol for Leo resembles the Uraeus serpent, worn on the head-dress of Egyptian pharaohs. It is related to the flow of energy in the universe, the land or in a human being, thus linking all things. In Sumerian mythology the primal creative mother goddess Nammu is seen both as a serpent and as the flowing waters of the ocean. Under the patriarchal influence of the later Babylonian civilization she becomes the demon-dragon, Tiamat, and later still the 'evil' serpent of Genesis. The Tarot attribution of Teth is Strength.

Yod (Jod) Phonetic value - I. Numerical value - 10

Yod is important as the first letter of the Tetragrammaton, corresponding to the creative energy of Chokmah. Pictorially and symbolically it represents the hand, the means of action and creation.

Yod is one of the 'simple' letters, and is associated with Virgo and sexuality. Its Tarot attribution is the Hermit.

Kaph Numerical value - 20
This letter is the fourth 'double', with the opposing meanings of abundance and scarcity, and a planetary correspondence with Jupiter. Its shape and interpretation relate to the palm of the hand, the part of the body which transmits the powerful but subtle energy used both in the martial arts and in spiritual healing.

The cardinal direction corresponding to Kaph is the west. In the Tarot it relates to the Wheel of Fortune.

Lamed Numerical value - 30
Lamed is another of the 'simple' letters, and is attributed to Libra and the human ability to work.

With its meaning of ox-goad, an implement for prodding cattle to make them move, Lamed symbolizes the power and initiative needed to set things in motion. In the Tarot it corresponds to the Justice card.

Mem Numerical value - 40
Mem is the second of the three creative 'mother' letters, and corresponds to the element of water and to the winter season. In the human body it rules the stomach.

The letter meaning is also associated with water, and therefore rules flowing, continuous change and rhythms, including birth, death and rebirth. The Tarot attribution of Mem is the Hanged Man, symbolizing transformation.

Nun Numerical value - 50
This is the eighth 'simple' letter, associated with Scorpio and the faculty of movement. The meaning of Nun is a fish, a creature whose habitat is water, linking this letter to Mem.

Nun is associated with the Tarot card of Death and with Scorpio, the sign ruling death, which also relates to the previous letter.

Samech Numerical value - 60
Samech is the nineth 'simple' letter, associated with Sagittarius and the faculty of anger. Its meaning is a prop, a thing which gives support. Therefore, the letter signifies the interdependence between the person or thing offering support at any level and who or what is being supported.

Samech corresponds to the Tarot card of Temperence.

Ayin Phonetic value - O. Numerical value - 70
Ayin is the tenth 'simple' letter, related to the sign of Capricorn and the human faculty of humour. Its meaning is an eye, linking the inner and outer realms, and denoting the power to perceive the deeper nature of things.

Ayin's Tarot attribution is the Devil.

Pe Numerical value - 80
Pe is the fifth 'double' letter, related to the dual qualities of grace and sinfulness. In shape and interpretation this character is associated with the mouth, which symbolizes eloquence and also the creative word spoken by the biblical god, the source of all existence. The Egyptian letter 'r' has a similar meaning.

Pe relates to the cardinal direction of north and to the planet Mars. Its Tarot attribution is the Tower.

Tzaddi Phonetic value - Tz. Numerical value - 90

This character is linked to Aquarius and the faculty of imagination, and is the eleventh 'simple' letter.

The meaning of the letter is a fish hook, the tool which enables a fish to bo taken from the water onto land. In relation to this, Tzaddi symbolizes the connecting links between things in different elements or dimensions.

In the Tarot it relates to the Star, or according to some sources to the Emperor.

Qoph Numerical value - 100
As the twelfth 'simple' letter, Qoph relates to the sign of Pisces and the ability to sleep. Qoph's meaning is the back of the head, which cannot be observed by a person except through a mirror. In a similar way mystical illumination is not directly accessible through the earthly senses, giving Qoph its symbolic interpretation. In the Tarot Qoph's attribution is the Moon.

Resh Numerical value - 200
Resh is the sixth 'double' letter, associated with fercundity and barrenness. It links with the above letter, Qoph, due to its meaning of the head, the seat of the intellect and the part of the body which gives manifestation to the light of human consciousness. It also incorporates the following letter, Shin.

Resh relates to the cardinal direction of south, and to both the planet and the Tarot trump of the Sun.

Shin Phonetic value - Sh. Numerical value - 300
Shin, the third and last of the 'mother' letters, relates to the element of fire.

This character represents a tooth, and is therefore linked to consuming and devouring. Chewing changes food into edible consistency, just as fire, Shin's ruling element, devours and transforms. On a higher level the fire of the divine spirit brings transformation.

Seasonally Shin represents the summer, while its Tarot attribution is the Judgement card.

Tau Phonetic value - Th. Numerical value - 400

This is the seventh and final 'double' letter, signifying both power and powerlessness. Its planetary attribution is Saturn, which in turn links it to the element of earth.

In shape Tau forms the cross of sacrifice, which makes up the lower portion of the Egyptian Ankh, symbol of eternal life.

Of the seven directions Tau corresponds to the centre, while in the Tarot it is linked to the trump of The World, signifying completion.

Mystical Insights through the use of Letters

According to Qabalistic doctrine the Hebrew scriptures contain hidden wisdom given by Yaweh, which can be decoded through applying the correct techniques. The three methods used to unveil this wisdom are known as Gematria, Notarikon and Temurah.

Each Hebrew letter has a numerical equivalent, because in ancient times the letters were used for mundane mathematical calculations as well as for writing. This pairing of letters and numbers makes it possible to employ the art of Gematria, in which the numerical equivalent of a word or phrase is calculated.

Words or phrases with the same total number are then believed to be mystically connected, so that divine messages and prophesies for the future are found concealed in the sacred texts. For example:

AChD meaning 'unity' is added as follows:

A = 1

Ch = 8

D = 4   Total= 13

which equates with 'love', spelt AHBH in Hebrew:

A = 1

H = 5

B = 2

H = 5   Total=13

Qabalists would therefore take this to mean that the nature of unity is love. To continue, JHVH adds as follows:

J = 10

H = 5

V = 6

H = 5   Total = 26

As the total of JHVH is double that of the two previous words this is taken to mean that Jehovah is unity manifested in duality.

Though the numbers being compared are often exact, the system of Gematria does allow for a difference of one between the totals of two linked words or phrases, a tradition referred to as 'colel'.

Notarikon is the second Qabalistic technique for decoding hidden esoteric messages from the scriptures. With this method the first and last letters of a word can be used to form another word, alternatively the letters of a single word can be used as the initial or last letters of every word in a phrase. Notarikon can also be used like Gematria to establish meaningful connections between words or sentences.

The final method of letter manipulation is called Temurah, and involves replacing one letter, or more, by another, in this way creating a text decipherable only by those who know the code.

The esoteric technique of Gematria and the correspondences associated with the Hebrew letters, especially those of the Tetragrammaton, are based on the Qabalistic theory that all things are interconnected, and more importantly that nothing can be separated from its root in the primal creative word, which continues to vibrate through the universe. For this reason the correspondences were, and still are, widely employed in ritual magic.

Chapter Four

Word-Masters and Wood-Sages

The ancient Celtic tradition was an oral one, where history, law and religious doctrine were transmitted from one generation to the next, from teacher to pupil, and committed to memory. It was presided over by the Druids, the ruling caste in Britain and Gaul, who kept all forms of knowledge under their tight control. Though the Druids and the Celtic aristocracy were able to write using the Greek alphabet it went against their beliefs to disseminate wisdom in this way and writing was used only for account keeping, inscriptions and mundane messages. So, unlike the ancient Egyptians, Greeks or Romans, the early Celts do not communicate to us directly, through their own words written in their own time. Instead, we have to rely on second hand reports and speculation.

A considerable amount of information comes to us through the writings of various Roman authors, such as Julius Ceasar and Tacitus though, as these writers were commenting on the ways of an enemy people, their observations are not always entirely objective! Details about early Celtic life is also known from archaeology, and from myth and legend, though this again is not objective and has undergone many alterations due to the original Pagan tales having been written down centuries later by Christian monks.

Written or spoken, the Celts were strongly aware of the magical potential of the word, a potential not only connected to words of power used in ritual but also to eloquence, storytelling and satire. The word could work on the mind and emotions, enabling those with sufficient skill to move or manipulate at all levels. Mystical poetry and song sustained the sacred land itself, while at the other end of the spectrum satire was said to be capable of literally destroying an enemy - again the word both gives and takes, preserves or harms.

Later, magical alphabets were employed, the Druids who used them going to great lengths to ensure secrecy, the very nature of these cryptic systems and their correspondences enhancing their power. The more recent of these alphabets use Latin characters, and are associated with beliefs about the creative word derived from the Bible, where the name of the biblical god gave rise to all life.

The Celts - Historical Background

The Celts have long been a source of fascination, ever since Roman times, the aura of mystery due to their lack of early written records adding to this. They are impossible to pin down, their earthly origins clouded by uncertainty, and the accounts of their religion only fragmentary. What is known, or assumed, about their beliefs tends to confuse the modern mind, nothing ever being quite what it seems, where the Otherworld is interwoven with this, everywhere and nowhere.

Even the word Celt illustrates their elusiveness. Its meaning is uncertain but according to some sources it is said to derive from 'Keltoi', meaning 'hidden ones'.

To the ancient Greeks the term 'Celt' applied to the European peoples living north of the Mediterranean, who were regarded by classical authors as barbarians. And, though they possessed a distinctive identity, they were a people united by culture and language rather than by ethnic roots. While historians still disagree as to their origins, most believe that the Celts spread west from eastern Europe in several waves, conquering and settling land from Iberia to Ireland.

Some scholars are of the opinion that Celtic culture had already developed by 2000 BC, though archaeologically the Celts first make themselves known through finds from near Lake Hallstatt in Austria, where the community led a life centred around salt-mining, farming and trading. It is after this site that the earliest phase of Celtic history is named, lasting from c.800 BC to around the mid-sixth century BC, with roots probably stretching as far back as c.1200 BC, and spanning the transition from the Bronze to the Iron Age. After the discovery of the site Celtic culture reflecting the same style and stage of development elsewhere in Europe was defined as Hallstatt, even when the finds are of a much later date.

The second phase of Celtic civilization is referred to as La Téne, after the village and votive deposits found at Lake Neuchâtel in Switzerland, dating from around 500 BC. Examples of La Téne design, the finest flowering of Celtic art, have also been found in many areas, reflecting the Celts at the height of their power as they swept across Europe. These are the Celts of popular imagination, heroic and flamboyant, who sacked Rome in 390 BC, and in 279 BC plundered the Greek oracular centre of Delphi.

Though they were fierce and warlike, this contrasted with the Celtic love of music, art and poetry, all of which played an important part in their culture. Even war was seen as an art-form, with the warriors boasting of their prowess in battle and the Bards making songs to immortalize the heroes.

Classical writers reporting on the Celts tell how they used the voice as a weapon in battle, uttering terrifying cries as they launched the attack. And in the Irish saga of 'Tain Bo Cuailgne' ('The Cattle Raid of Cooley') the Ulster warrior Cuchulainn employs chants to empower himself in combat.

However, in the end the Celts' romantic attitude to war contributed to their downfall, when courageous but comparatively unorganized warriors met with the highly regimented Roman troops. Another contributory factor was the

Celtic inability to unite as one people rather than warring amongst themselves, one clan against another.

Celtic culture may have existed in the British Isles as early as the second millenium BC, evolving and being enriched by small groups of invaders, rather than through a full-scale conquest of Britain from the Continent. The newcomers blended with the indigenous island peoples, absorbing some of their belief systems and merging them with their own. This process is thought by many to be the origin of druidry, a combination of British Bronze Age or earlier Neolithic rites and Indo-European religion, the former centered around stone circles and the practice of shamanism.

During the Roman occupation of mainland Britain the Celts became Romanized to a certain extent, though their own cultural identity was never lost. Finally, as a result of the Anglo-Saxon invasions in the fifth century AD, the native British were driven west into Somerset, Devon, Cornwall and Wales, and also across the Channel to Brittany, taking their myths and traditions with them.

Language

The language in which these myths were first told belongs to the Indo-European group and is one of the factors which defines the Celts as a people. The two main forms, referred to as Q-Celtic and P-Celtic, which have evolved from the original tongue possess many similarities, but also certain marked differences. The former is spoken by Goidelic or Gaelic Celts and retains the Indo-European 'q', written as 'c' and pronounced with the hard sound of 'k'. In the second, P-Celtic or Brythonic, the 'q' or 'c' sound becomes a 'p'. Therefore, the word for head, 'cenn' in Goidelic, becomes 'penn' in Brythonic. Similarly, the Goidelic mac, meaning 'son of', appears as the Welsh map or mab. In Welsh the 'm' and sometimes also the 'a' is dropped, giving such names as Pritchard.

Goidelic Celts travelled to the far west of Europe at an earlier date than the Brythons, and their branch of the language is found in Ireland, the Isle of Man and Scotland, which was settled by Gaelic speakers in the fifth century AD. Brythonic was spoken in many areas of Celtic Europe, including Gaul, and later developed into Cornish, Welsh and Breton.

Druids and Bards

Ancient Celtic society was presided over by the Druid caste, who acted as priests, judges, philosophers, doctors and astronomers, to name but a few of their many vital roles. As was the case with scribes in ancient Egypt the Druids' unique place in society is shown by the fact that they were exempt from taxes, and the honour-price for maiming or killing a Druid (ie. the amount that had to be paid by the culprit) was extremely high.

Classical authors commenting on the Druids also remark on the high status of Bards and Ovates, indicating that these were most likely two of the many vocations which were followed by those of the Druid caste. In this chapter I use the word Bard as a generic term for a a person fulfilling the role of sacred poet, except in specific references to Ireland.

As shown in ancient Celtic myth, Bards were masters of words of power. They were highly trained in both the literary arts and in magic, and could combine the two for beneficial purposes or in a reportedly deadly cocktail. It is claimed that a satire against an enemy had sufficient power to bring about harm, such as causing black blotches to appear on a person's face, or even to kill. A Bard was also capable of affecting both the land and animals, ruining an enemy by causing barrenness. The traditional posture adopted for cursing was to stand on one foot, using one hand and one eye, a stance which is mentioned in many Irish myths. In the 'Book of Invasions' when the solar god Lugh fights with the Tuatha de Danaan for the conquest of Ireland he takes on the form of a misshapen hag 'with one leg, one hand, one eye', and in this position curses the enemy Fomorians.

A man could also be disgraced for life if criticised in a bardic satire for such things as cowardice or lack of hospitality. Again, an example occurs in the 'Book of Invasions', which tells how King Bres failed to provide comfortable accomodation for the Bard, Corpry, who then composed the following satire on him:

'Without food quickly served,

Without cow's milk whereon a calf can grow,

Without a dwelling fit for a man under the gloomy night,

Without means to entertain a bardic company,

Let such be the condition of Bres.'

Bres was so affected by the satire, which even undermined his physical health, that he was deemed unfit to rule and was forced to abdicate.

Every Celtic king or lord had his own Bard to recount his ancestry, compose poetry, sing his praises and mock his enemies. He also provided meaningful entertainment during the dark days of winter between Samhain and Beltane, the season for storytelling around the fire. In an oral tradition members of the Druid caste were the repository for all the information that we now have access to simply by opening a book or turning on a computer.

The Court Bard's heroic tales were of vital importance to the tribe's morale, giving a mythic potency to their history and deeds. The power of the word on the lips of a skilled Bard brought the gods, the land and the heroes of past and present vividly to life, making the listeners feel part of a greater whole, of a timeless, cyclical world, uplifting and inspiring them.

The Bards knew all about the nature of sonics, so by employing carefully devised rhythms and keys, they could profoundly affect their listeners. Everything was composed and performed with intent in order to produce the strongest impact: music, poetic modes and language.

During the Roman occupation of Europe and mainland Britain, when druidry was banned, the Druids adopted the role of Bard in order to escape persecution. They focussed outwardly on the musical and poetic side of their tradition whilst performing their other practices in secret. In Ireland, however, which was never conquered by the Romans the Druids continued to exist openly until the fifth century AD.

Later, when Christianity became the official religion of much of Continental Europe and of the British Isles the Druids' new identity, that of Bard in Wales and Fili (Filid - plural) in Ireland, was acceptable to the church as opposed to their original Pagan priestly functions. Some Druids also converted to being Christian monks, outwardly at least, and St Columba himself was trained as a Fili.

The associated grade of Ovate in Wales or Fáith (Fáithi - plural) in Ireland was responsible for divination and sacrifice, and in Ireland was later assimilated into the Filid, the function of sacrifice having been dropped. The roles of both Fili and Fřith were open to women, who were called respectively Bánfili and Bánfáith, and are mentioned in Irish myth.

In Ireland the highest grade of Filid was known as an Ollamh (Ollave), roughly the equivalent of a modern doctorate. As a sign of their prestige those who had reached this level were given expensive gifts such as fine horses and jewels, and they were entitled to a retinue of twenty- four men. The Ollamh's symbol of office was a gold branch hung with bells, while a Fili of between seven to nine years training carried a silver branch, and a lower grade of poet carried a bronze branch. These branches were shaken to announce that the Bard was about to perform, or to tell the Otherworld that a shaman was about to start his inner journeying to that realm. Symbolically the branch relates to that of the Otherworld tree where the birds of Rhiannon sang, transporting all who heard them into a dimension outside time.

7. A Bard, carrying the silver branch, symbolic of his calling

The branch also relates to the eternal tree growing in the Otherworld, representing the sacred and enduring nature of the bardic craft, the fertility of imagination and the timeless tradition, passed down through the generations.

An Irish Fili had to undergo training which lasted twelve years or more, during which time he memorized around 350 stories and a large number of poems, besides learning the use of secret alphabets and the composition of poetry, using specific metres.

All instruction was oral, often in the form of a teaching dialogue. The methods used by later bardic schools, some as recent as the eighteenth century in Scotland, give an insight as to the training the early Bards were subjected to. This involved lying in the dark, in some cases on the back with a stone on the stomach, with no distractions to interrupt the flow of poetic inspiration.

After the Christianisation of the Welsh Court Bards their poetry became very formalized and they were forbidden to use mythological themes, nor was love and nature poetry in favour. Instead, their main role was to compose religious verse or to praise their royal master. In Ireland, however, the Filid, were not so restricted and were still expected to use imagination combined with the obligatory technical skill.

Besides the formal Court Bards, who were attached to the households of lords, in Wales there was also a guild of itinerant Bards who travelled from place to place recounting mythological tales. They were also credited with powers of divination, prophesy and satire, similar to the ancient druidic Bards.

On the Continent in Medieval times wandering storytellers or conteurs also told traditional legends, involving heroes and kings from various tribes rather than those specific to one family. The Breton conteurs - mostly from British immigrant families - were regarded as the best. Minstrels performed the same role, preserving and recounting traditional material, combined with their own compositions.

In the twelfth and thirteenth centuries the courtly poets of southern France, northern Spain and Italy were known as troubadours. The first such was William of Aquitaine, Count of Poitiers, whose grand-daughter Eleanor of Aquitaine introduced the tradition to the courts of northern France, where it met with Breton legends. The merging of the two found written expression in the Arthurian tales, the earliest composed in the late twelfth century by Chrétien de Troyes, court poet to Eleanor's daughter, Marie de Champagne.

In Wales the itinerant Bards and minstrels found favour with Norman knights, who introduced them into their courts, and in the fourteenth century the Court Bards were again encouraged to compose love poetry, though satires were forbidden. The role of the Welsh Court Bard came to an end at the time of the Civil Wars, while Cromwell's conquest of Ireland destroyed the Irish Ollamhs.

In England Bards were never accorded the prestige of their highly trained counterparts in Wales and Ireland, though they still played an important role. The Medieval minstrel who was attached to a noble house wore the badge of his patron on a silver chain, while other minstrels were under the patronage of city corporations. They were part of a guild, identified by their livery and badge, and entertained the Mayor on state occasions. *The Merchants' Guild Book of Leicester* states that in 1481 'Henry Howman, a harper,' was made free of (ie. joined) the guild. Minstrels who had no such formal attachments were regarded as vagrants and punished as such, though the attitude towards them varied at different periods.

The bardic tradition, for centuries oral, passed down from generation to generation, was eventually preseved on paper, giving a unique insight into Celtic life and values. The earliest Irish texts date from the eigth century AD but most manuscripts containing mythology are Medieval. In Ireland the most well-known of these tales are: *The Book of Invasions* - twelfth century; *The Ulster Cycle*, including '*The Tain Bo Cuailgne*' from the twelfth century manuscript *The Book of the Dun Cow*, which was written in the Monastery of St Kieran; and the Ossianic Cycle, found in manuscripts of the eleventh and twelfth centuries.

Welsh mythology is preserved in the 'Triads' and in the *Mabinogion*, the latter written down between the eleventh and thirteenth centuries. *The Red Book of Hergest*, dating from around 1400, contains the earliest complete version of the *Mabinogion*, while the earlier *White Book of Rhydderch*, dating to around 1325, is incomplete.

As late as 1579 satire was, if not feared, regarded as a severe offence, punishable with death. Two Edinburgh poets, William Turnbull and William Scot, were hanged in that year for writing a satirical ballad directed against the Earl of Morton.

The minstrel class gradually dwindled, though Ben Jonson mentions the Chief Minstrel of Highgat, and, in an article entitled *Romance*, Sir Walter Scott writes that at around 1770 'a person acquired the nickname of 'Roswal and Lillian' from singing that romance about the streets of Edinburgh, which is probably the very last instance of the proper minstrel craft.' However, other writers of the eighteenth and nineteenth centuries mention minstrels in both England and Scotland, though they are a rarity. As late as the mid-nineteenth century a man named J H Dixon tells of the Yorkshire minstrels who led settled lives for the majority of the year, but travelled to perform traditional ballads at festival times such as Christmas.

In fact, the bardic art in its many guises had, and has, never died. In Celtic areas the occasional bardic school continued into the eighteenth century, the century when druidry and its associated bardcraft was 'revived' and became fashionable in certain artistic and learned circles. Modern Druid tradition states that in 1717 John Toland held a druidic meeting at the Apple Tree Tavern in Covent Garden, thereby bringing about the renaissance of the movement, though there is no concrete evidence that Toland was the father of the revival.

Another eighteenth century figure instrumental in bringing druidry, and especially bardcraft, to the fore was the Welshman Edward Williams (1747-1826), more commonly known by his bardic name of Iolo Morganwg. Probably with the aid of genuine documents in his possession, but mingled with a large amount of material from his own imagination, he compiled a number of manuscripts linking Welsh Bards to the ancient Druids, 'proving' that they descended through the ages in an unbroken line. His manuscripts were not suspected of being faked for many years, leading Iolo's Gorsedd ceremony to be included in the Welsh Eisteddfod, which possessed a genuinely long history.

Bardic contests had been taking place in Wales since before the time of King Hwl the Good, c.950, continuing in the Medieval period and sixteenth century. However, the tradition had lapsed until the modern Eisteddfod was founded in 1789, when Thomas Jones of Corwen organized a large regional gathering. This was followed by similar regional events, then in 1860 it was decided to hold a National Eidsteddfod each year, alternating between North and South Wales, a custom which still continues to this day as a focus for cultural activity.

Celtic mythology features several powerful Bards, whose names are still familiar to many people as archetypal of those following the vocation. Perhaps the most well-known name is that of Taliesin, both as a mythological character and as a real historical figure of the Dark Ages.

Taliesin the Bard

Lady Charlotte Guest's 1849 translation of *'The Mabinogion'* includes 'The Story of Taliesin', though this tale is found in a sixteenth century manuscript rather than in the 'Red Book of Hergest'. It tells of the miraculous birth of the Bard to Ceridwen, goddess of the Underworld, transformation and initiation. She is the crone or dark aspect of the Goddess, symbolized in Paganism by the dark moon, one who destroys in order to make way for the new, as the following tale shows:

Ceridwen had two children, a beautiful daughter named Creiwy and a son Avagddu, who had the misfortune to be terribly ugly. To make up for this Ceridwen decided to use her considerable magical skills to create a potion, three drops of which would bestow on him the gift of inspiration. As the cauldron of inspiration had to be kept boiling continuously for a year and a day, Ceridwen employed a blind man to tend the fire beneath it and a youth by the name of Gwion Bach to stir the contents.

One day, as he was carrying out his duties, three drops of boiling liquid from the cauldron fell on Gwion's finger and he put it in his mouth to cool it. Immediately he was filled with inspiration and prophetic knowledge. He realized what had happened and, knowing that he was in danger from Ceridwen, fled to his own land, while the cauldron which now contained only poison burst in two.

When Ceridwen discovered that all her efforts had been in vain she went in pursuit of Gwion who used his new-found skills to turn himself into a hare, whereupon Ceridwen turned herself into a hound. Gwion then transformed himself into a fish, and Ceriwen as an otter continued the pursuit. When Gwion tried to escape by taking the form of a small bird Ceridwen became a hawk. Finally, Gwion turned himself into a wheat grain, which Ceridwen, now in the form of a hen, swallowed.

Nine months later she gave birth to a baby boy and, though she had intended to kill him, could not carry out her intent because of his beauty. Instead she placed him in a leather bag and threw it into the sea on Beltane eve. A previously luckless man named Elphin fished up the bag at his father's salmon weir, where the man who tended the weir saw the child's beautiful forehead and said, 'Behold a radiant brow!' to which Elphin replied, 'Taliesin be he called'. He and his wife adopted the boy, from which time they prospered due to the child's phenomenal bardic skills.

On one occasion Taliesin, still a youth, went to the court of King Maelgwn of Gwynedd who had taken Elphin prisoner for boasting about his wife and his Bard. By placing his finger against his pouted lips Taliesin made the sound 'blerwn', rendering the royal Bards incapable of doing anything else but creating the same sound. He then contested with Maelgwn's chief Bard for Elphin's freedom, his song finally causing a fierce wind. When his foster father was brought from the dungeon Taliesin's song was so powerful that it broke the chains which bound him.

Due to Taliesin's legendary birth, the ancient Bards regarded Ceridwen as their mother and patroness. The above tale symbolizes the secret initation into the bardic order, re-birth through Ceridwen's cauldron, and all who aspired to the Welsh bardic chair had to 'taste the waters of inspiration' contained within it.

As to Taliesin himself, there was a historical Bard of this name who flourished in the sixth century, who is the composer of twelve eulogies or praise poems in honour of several royal patrons, including Urien of Rheged and his son Owein, warlords fighting for their native lands against the Anglo-Saxon advances.

The eulogies are to be found in the late thirteenth century manuscript known as *The Book of Taliesin*, which also contains a large body of poetry involving shamanism, druidic lore and magic. The latter is almost certainly not composed by Taliesin the eulogist, instead it is the product of an oral tradition with its roots stretching back hundreds of years, but not recorded in written form until Medieval times. It may even preserve the remains of ancient bardic practices from before the Roman conquest. The name of the great Bard has been attached to such poems in order to emphasize their importance amongst later followers of the tradition, who were working to ensure its continuity. It is also more than possible that Taliesin was not in fact a personal name but a title given to someone who had reached a certain stage of bardic or druidic initiation. This body of work includes the influential poem 'Cad Goddeu' or 'Battle of the Trees', with its many levels of meaning, which may have been used to teach the lore of wisdom and poetry.

Finn MacCumhaill

In many ways similar to the Welsh tale of Taliesin, the Irish story of Finn MacCumhaill expains how he gained his exceptional powers:

Beside the Well of Segais at the source of the River Boyne grew nine hazel trees, their nuts bestowing poetic inspiration and wisdom. And on these nuts Fintan, the Salmon of Wisdom, fed, absorbing their power.

As a youth the warrior-hero Finn, then still known by his childhood name of Deimne, went to learn the bardic art from Finneces 'white wisdom' on the banks of the Boyne.

For seven years the elder Bard had sought the Salmon of Wisdom as it had been prophesied that he and no other would gain universal knowledge from eating the fish. When eventually the salmon was caught, Finneces gave Deimne the task of cooking it, warning his pupil not to eat any of it. But, despite this warning Deimne put his thumb in his mouth when he was scalded by a drop of hot fish oil, thus gaining the wisdom himself. Without reprimanding him, Finneces acknowledged that the prophesy concerned Deimne all along and gave him his true name of Finn, meaning 'fair one'.

Thereafter Finn only had to put his thumb in his mouth in order to perceive all things.

The gift of bardic inspiration and the skills of a warrior are combined in Finn, showing that both forms of power are equally valid, as illustrated by the dual nature of the god Oghma. In order to join Finn's warrior brotherhood, the Fianna, it was necessary for the candidate to know the Twelve Books of Poetry and to be able to compose perfect verse in the bardic tradition, as well as displaying military skills.

Finn's son Oisin (Ossian) also combined the skills of warrior and poet, and is the traditional author of the Ossianic Cycle of tales.

Amergin

Also in Irish mythology, in *'The Book of Invasions'* we meet Amergin, Chief Bard and advisor to the Gaels, or Milesians. According to the tale Ireland was conquered by successive waves of races, the last being the Gaels who hailed from Spain and reached Ireland at Beltane. Amergin, meaning 'Wonderful Mouth', was at the forefront of the conquerers and the moment he stepped onto dry land he spoke the following poem, forming mystic links with the natural powers of his new territory:

> *'I am a wind of the sea,*
>
> *I am a wave of the sea,*
>
> *I am a sound of the sea,*
>
> *I am a stag of seven tines,*
>
> *I am a hawk on a cliff,*
>
> *I am a tear of the sun,*
>
> *I am fair among flowers,*
>
> *I am a boar,*
>
> *I am a salmon in a pool,*
>
> *I am a lake on a plain,*
>
> *I am a hill of poetry,*
>
> *I am a battle-waging spear,*
>
> *I am a god who forms fire for a head.'*

The Milesians then proceeded to the royal seat of Tara, where they demanded that the three kings of Ireland surrender their territory. Amergin honourably declared that the Milesians would not take their foes by surprise, but instead would sail out beyond the nineth wave and return to give battle. However, the Danaans who already occupied the land did not play fair and raised a magical mist and tempest, which obscured the coast from view. As a Bard, Amergin was able to use the mighty power of the word to assist his people and he chanted the following incantation to Erin, requesting her help:

'I invoke the land of Ireland,

Shining, shining sea;

Fertile, fertile mountain;

Gladed, gladed wood!

Abundant river, abundant in water!

Fish-abounding lake!'

The mists then cleared and the tempest dropped, so the Milesians were able to head towards the shore and take possession of their new home.

Bride - Fire of Inspiration

In ancient Ireland, the goddess who ruled the fire of the hearth and of the smith's forge was also the lady who ignited the flame of poetic inspiration. She was the divine muse of the Bards, patroness of the affiliated art of divination, and the giver of wisdom.

Bride, whose name derives from the word for 'bright', was the daughter of the Irish father god, the Dagda, and is often depicted in triple form, her other aspects governing healing and smithcraft. Just as weapons were skillfully crafted, so too were poetic compositions. Similarly, her role as goddess of fertility can be related not only to physical reproduction but also to artistic and bardic creativity, as all arts and crafts were under her guidance.

Oghma, the Honey-Mouthed

Another Irish deity who presided over the gift of poetic inspiration was the mighty Oghma, credited with inventing the sacred Ogham Script. He also governed art, music, magic, physical strength and eloquence, giving him the appellation 'honey-mouthed'.

In one Romano-Celtic representation, mentioned by the Greek author Lucian of Samosata, fine chains linked Oghma's tongue to

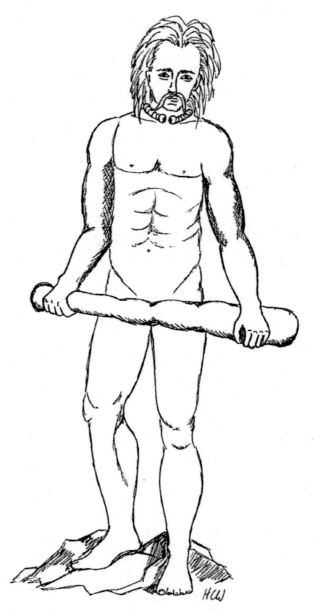

8. Oghma - eloquence is mightier than a warrior's strength

the ears of humans, who were symbolically bound by his words. And, like Hercules, he was depicted carrying a huge club, indicating his role as champion of the Tuatha de Danaan. Though the two roles of warrior and Bard may seem contradictory, both held power and prestige in Celtic society. Words could be used as a weapon with as much effect as Oghma's club, and it has often been shown that 'the pen is mightier than the sword'. The power of his word to create, inspire or destroy are the marks of his true strength.

Oghma married Etan, daughter of the physician god Diancecht, with whom he had several children. One of these, Cairpre, came to occupy the important position of Bard to the Tuatha de Danaan.

Sacred Alphabets

Ogham - The Celtic Tree Alphabet
A fifteenth century manuscript 'The Book of Ballymote' is the chief work on the subject of Ogham, and the source of the myth concerning its invention by the god of eloquence.

In Ogham the letters are represented by combinations of strokes, written above, below or across a line, known in Irish as the 'druim'. Where this line is vertical the letters run from bottom to top, and where it is horizontal from left to right. On a pillar stone, the corner between two of the stone's surfaces is taken as the 'druim'.

Some scholars claim that the system dates back as far as c.2200 BC, a theory based on finds of Bronze Age chalk slabs which show markings resembling Ogham signs. More conservative estimates date the earliest inscriptions to the second century AD.

Inscriptions in Ogham are found on pillar stones mainly in Ireland, though examples also exist in Scotland and Wales, and a few in England and Continental Europe. These usually bear

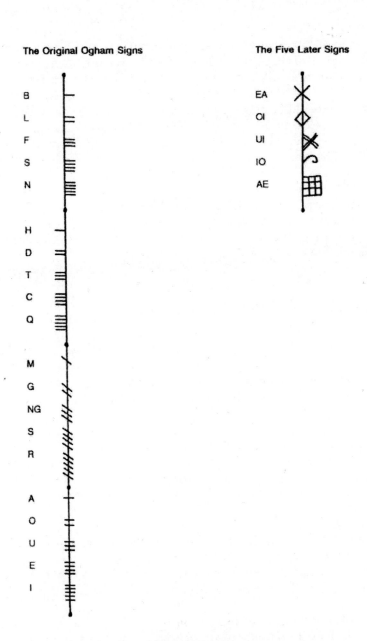

The Ogham Alphabet

memorial inscriptions or dedications to the gods. A second, and important, use for Ogham was in the magical arts, where it was employed for secret communication and divination, engraved on wooden staves rather than on large pillar stones. Thirdly, it was used as a key to open the inner store-house of bardic memory through a series of correspondences.

Originally there were twenty letters, with a further five added at a later date, each associated with a tree, the letter value being equivalent to the initial of the tree name. There is also a widely-used system which relates each letter not only to a tree but to a lunar month. This theory was put forward by the poet Robert Graves from his interpretation of the poem *'Cad Goddeu'* and scholars tell us that there is no previous record of a tree calendar in Celtic tradition, though there would have been seasonal tree lore.

Etymologically wood and wisdom are often linked in Celtic languages; the Irish word for trees is 'fid' and for knowledge 'fios', while in Wales 'gwydd' means trees and 'gwyddon' knowledge-able one. This links to the probable origin of the word Druid, 'drui' in Irish and 'derwydd' in Welsh, combining the word for oak, 'daur' in Irish and 'derw' in Welsh, with knowledge, giving a wise man of the oak or wood-sage.

Metaphors concerning wood-carving to describe the composition of poetry have also been used by Bards since Taliesin's time or earlier. However, during the Roman occupation (43-410 AD) Druids began keeping mundane records on materials such as goat skin parchment and on a form of paper made from flax.

The Mysteries of Ogham

Ogham was manipulated in many ways in order to make it comprehensible only to druidic initiates, for example Ogham Consaine used only consonants, one or more of which could be replaced with another or others.

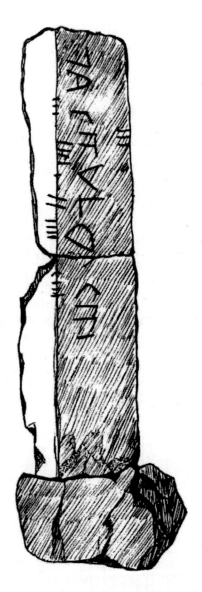

9. An Ogham stone from Lewannick, Cornwall, bearing a dual inscription in Ogham and Latin which reads 'Here lies Ulcagnus'.

Other cryptic systems are akin to the tree alphabet, but use alternative objects or places to describe the letters. These include Bird Ogham, using the name of a bird which has a name beginning with the relevant letter, Lin Ogham, using the names of lakes and pools, and Ceall (Battle) Ogham, using the initial letter of a weapon or other object with military associations. Such systems enabled initiates to speak in code, using lists of birds, etc to spell words. Also, animals, birds, lakes etc, denoting letters could be used in poetry, giving it both a mundane and an esoteric meaning. In a similar way, Muc (colour) Ogham allowed hidden wisdom to be encoded in coloured patterns and artwork.

A Bard had to understand all the complex relationships between the letters of an inscription, and their many secret meanings. No letter was merely incidental, but each had a precise puropse.

Another way in which initiates used Ogham was for secret sign language. Sron Ogham involved using the fingers to form the letter signs, with the nose-bone as the druim. In Coir Ogham the fingers were placed across the foot or shinbone in order to spell words, while Bar Ogham involved placing the fingers of one hand across the other.

The Ogham system known as Finn's Window, named after the legendary poet and hero, is illustrated in the *Book of Ballymote*, and shows the Ogham letters arranged around a wheel, making correspondences with the cardinal and inter-cardinal points of the compass.

The magical use of Ogham is shown in the *Tain Bo Cuailgne* when Cuchulainn uses it to bind the warriors of Queen Maev. He adopts the traditional cursing posture, standing on one leg and using only one hand and one eye, then cuts an oak sapling and bends it into a circular shape. This he carves with Ogham symbols, describing how it was made, and leaves it around a pillar stone in the path of the advancing armies. He puts them under geis (taboo) not to pass the stone until the script has been deciphered and one of the enemy warriors has constructed a similar item by exactly the same means.

Letter	Irish Name	Tree	Welsh Name	Month
B	beith	birch	bedwen	24 Dec/20 Jan
L	luis	rowan	cerdinen	21 Jan/17 Feb
F/V	fearn	alder	gwernen	*18 Mar/14 Apr
S	saille	willow	helygen	*15 Apr/12 May
N	nuin	ash	onnen	*18 Feb/17 Mar

*I have written these in the usual letter sequence, rather than in Robert Graves' calendar sequence.

Letter	Irish Name	Tree	Welsh Name	Month
H	huathe	hawthorn	draenen wen	13 May/9 June
D	duir	oak	derwen/dar	10 June/7 July
T	tinne	holly	celynnen	8 July/4 Aug
C/K	coll	hazel	collen	5 Aug/1 Sep
Q	quert	apple	afal	Shares month with Coll
M	muinn	vine	gwinwydden	2 - 29 September
G	gort	ivy	eiddew, iorwg	30 Sep/27 Oct
NG	ngetal	broom/fern	eithin/rhedynen	28 Oct/24 Nov
STR/Z	straif	blackthorn	draenen ddu	Shares month with Saille
R	ruis	elder	ysgawen	25 Nov up to Solstice
A	ailm	silver fir/pine	ffynidwydden/ pinwydden	Extra Day after Winter Solstice
O	onn	gorse	eithin	
U	ur	heather	grug	
E	edhadh	aspen	aethnen	
I/J/Y	ido	yew	ywen	Winter Solstice

The Later Signs

Letter	Irish Name	Tree	Welsh Name
EA	edhadh	aspen	aethnen
OI	oir	spindle tree	piswydden
UI	uileand	honeysuckle	gywddfid
IO	iphin	gooseberry	eirin Mair
AE	phagos	beech	ffawydden

The Ogham Tree Alphabet

98

Divination

Another use for Ogham was in divination, when the letters would be inscribed on small pieces of wood and cast in order to obtain an answer, such as learning the sex of an unborn child. It was also used to discover whether a person was guilty of a crime if there were no witnesses.

The Gaelic Alphabet

As in Ogham, each letter of the Gaelic alphabet is linked with a tree, apart from two, fire and garden, teine (holly in the Ogham version) and gart, while yew occurs twice.

However, the Gaelic alphabet uses Roman letters rather than Ogham signs, and also follows the sequence of the Roman alphabet, starting with A - fhalm - elm. There are seventeen letters plus H, which is regarded as an accent, each corresponding with a number.

Interpretation of the Ogham Letters

Beith - Birch

The birch is a tree of beginnings, the first to sprout new leaves in spring, just as the white colour of its trunk symbolizes cleansing and purity. Switches made from its wood were once used for exorcising evil spirits from lunatics and for banishing the spirit of the old year. It indicates that the past must be left behind, along with all outworn trends.

Luis - Rowan

The rowan has always been regarded as a charm against bewitchment, and sprigs used to be fixed over byre doors to protect cattle. In Wales rowan trees were once grown in churchyards to guard the dead, instead of the more usual yew tree, while ancient Irish belief claimed that a rowan stake driven through a corpse would stop its ghost from wandering. Also in Irish legend, rowan berries were said to have the property of healing the wounded and of extending a man's life by a year.

The rowan had many magical purposes. Druids summoned spirits over fires of rowan wood and rowan trees were often to be found in the proximity of ancient stone circles. Though hazel rods were used for finding water, rods made of rowan were considered the best for metal divining.

Fearn - Alder
Because the alder grows in moist areas it has oily, water-resistant timber, suitable for underwater building foundations. In the Welsh myth of 'Branwen Daughter of Llyr', the god Bran used his own body as a bridge over the River Linon to raise his followers above its waters, thus linking him to this tree.

The same myth tells how Bran's severed head possessed the gift of prophesy, an association which extends to his sacred tree. There is also a link between fire and alder, shown by the tragic incident when Bran's nephew Gwern, meaning alder, is thrown into the fire.

Saille - Willow
The willow is the tree of the Goddess in her dark aspect, ruling the waning moon, magic and witchcraft, which according to some sources derives its name from an early word for willow. It is found near water, which is affected by the moon's phases.

The salicin in the bark of the willow is used to cure diseases common in damp areas, such as rheumatism, once believed to be caused by witchcraft.

Nuin - Ash
In Celtic belief the ash links the three circles of being: Abred, Gwynfydd and Ceugant, similar in concept to the Norse world tree, Yggdrasil. Its wood was used for druidic wands, such as the one found on Anglesey bearing a spiral design.

The ash was associated with the power of water, its timber forming the oars and spars of Irish and Welsh coracles, and the wood of a sacred ash was considered an effective charm against drowning.

Huathe - Hawthorn

The hawthorn is the tree of Beltane, the only day when it can be cut to form garlands for decorating houses and maypoles, honouring the Green Lady of summer fertility and her consort. The hawthorn is also known as whitethorn, due to its pale bark, and may, from its time of flowering.

According to Robert Graves, the orgiastic associations of May and its tree were first brought to Britain in the 1st century BC, and it was formerly linked with celibacy and the dark aspect of the Goddess. The Greeks and Romans believed it was unlucky to marry in May, the month of purification before the Midsummer festival. Therefore, the hawthorn represents cleansing and chastity.

Duir - Oak

The oak is the tree of male power, of the sun at the height of its strength at the Summer Solstice. This festival marks the end of the season of the symbolic Oak King, the waxing of the year when nature brings forth lush greenery. After his reign is ended he is sacrificed by burning, in later times simply by the burning of the wood, but according to J G Frazer in *The Golden Bough* human sacrifice may once have been involved.

The oak is often struck by lightning, hence its association with fire and fire gods, symbolizing divine light and inspiration coming to earth. To the Druids the oak was the most sacred of all trees, their very name probably deriving from it. They celebrated their rites in oak groves, and the power which continued to be associated with this tree led Edward the Confessor to preach under the Gospel Oak on Parliament Hill, Hampstead.

Due to the oak's endurance and the solidity of its timber, it symbolizes strength and security, while its solar associations bring inner spirituality.

Tinne - Holly

After the Summer Solstice the reign of the Holly King, the waning of the vegetational year begins, lasting until the Winter Solstice. As the holly defends itself with its sharp leaves, and spear shafts were fashioned from its wood, it was regarded as a fighter. Hence, this tree represents the ability to protect oneself spiritually and materially.

Coll - Hazel

In Irish mythology, Fintan, the Salmon of Wisdom, gained his powers from the nuts dropped by nine hazel trees into the Well of Segais at the source of the River Boyne. Finn MacCumhaill (Coll), meaning son of the hazel, in turn obtained his poetic skill and wisdom from eating the fish, which had absorbed the hazel's gifts.

Finn's shield, made of hazel wood, killed enemy warriors by its toxic vapours, symbolically representing the deadly satiric poem of which the Bard was a master.

Hazel rods were used not only for water divining, but also to discover if a man was guilty of committing a serious crime. Carrying a hazel rod was also believed to render a person invisible.

Quert - Apple

Apples are associated in myth with the Otherworld and immortality, as in the Arthurian legends where the wounded king is taken to the Isle of Avalon by nine fairy women, there to remain until his land has need of him. Afal is the Welsh for apple, after which the mystic isle is named.

In Norse mythology, eating the apples of the goddess Idun brought immortality to the gods. And the Greek Hesperides, daughters of Hesperus, god of the west, were the guardians of magical golden apples which Hercules had to find as one of his twelve labours.

A possible reason why the apple has gained these associations is that if its core is cut horizontally across it shows a pentagram, symbol of man, magic, protection and spiritual aspiration.

Muinn - Vine
Both the vine and the ivy grow in a spiral, the symbol for death and rebirth, thus linking the vine with resurrection. As the tree sacred to Dionysus, it has the properties of joy, divine intoxication and wrath.

The vine brings prophetic powers, the ability to escape the restrictions of the logical mind, allowing instinct and deeper emotions to surface.

Gort - Ivy
Like the vine, ivy grows spirally, representing death and resurrection, life and death in balance, the spiral of life, the Wheel of Fortune, and the search for the self.

Also like the vine, ivy is sacred to Dionysus. Its sacrificial aspect is shown in the myth of the king of the waxing year, symbolized by the robin, who kills the king of the waning year, the gold crest wren, which is hiding in an ivy bush.

Ngetal - Reed
The straight reed was a plant from which arrows were made. Therefore, it represents a clear sense of purpose, a positive direct approach to what a person aims to do in life, and the ability to overcome obstacles.

Egyptian pharaohs used reed sceptres, making it a royal symbol in the eastern Mediterranean.

Straif - Blackthorn
This is a winter tree with black bark, and its fruit, the sloe berry, ripens only after the first frosts. The wood was used for the Irish cudgel or for witches' staffs, and the thorns for pricking wax images in magic. Because of these associations the blackthorn is regarded as an unlucky tree, and it is possibly the origin of the word 'strife'.

Ruis - Elder
Elder represents the dying of the year, the winding down period. It is the tree of the crone goddess, associated with witches and death. Jesus was supposedly crucified on a cross of elder wood, and according to folk tradition it is considered unlucky to burn elder logs in the fire.

Ailm - Silver Fir
The silver fir is sacred to the triple moon goddess. In many traditions it is associated with birth, and Robert Graves' tree calendar assigns this tree to the birthday of the Son of Light, the divine child, on 'the extra day of the Winter Solstice'.

Onn -Furze
The furze has bright yellow flowers in spring, symbolic of the young solar god. As it attracts the first bees of the year it is regarded as propitious, and in Wales the furze is used as a charm against witches.

Ur - Heather
Heather is associated with midsummer, its flowers the red of passion. As a summer plant, it is also associated with bees, which the early Celts regarded as messengers between worlds. The three magical rays of light cast at the Solstice sunrise open

the gates of the Otherworld and represent the druidic Awen - illumination-inspiration.

Edhadh - White Poplar, also known as Aspen

This tree gives the ability to endure and conquer, and in Latin myth Hercules wreathed his head with poplar after he had killed the giant Cacus. Shields used to be made from its wood, thus it symbolically protects.

The poplar is linked with speech due to its affinity with the wind, as the leaves are so shaped that they 'whisper' when stirred. Many ancient cultures believed that the voices of the gods or spirits were carried on the wind.

Ido - Yew

The yew is regarded as a death tree, and is usually found planted in graveyards, to stop the dead from haunting the living and to protect them against graverobbers.

Yews can live to a great age, over two thousand years. Their branches grow down into the ground to form stems, which in turn become the trunks of new but connected growth. Therefore, when the original trunk decays a new tree is flourishing within the remains of the old. This property makes the yew not only a tree of death but of rebirth, associated with resurrection in Christian belief. On Robert Graves' tree calendar it is placed on the last day of the solar year, the day of death, before the sun/son is reborn.

Bardic Belief

The Three Rays

The Welsh texts known as *Barddas*, compiled from the works of Iolo Morganwg, tell how the universe came into existence by the creator speaking his own name. Morganwg may have gained his information from actual ancient manuscripts, or may simply

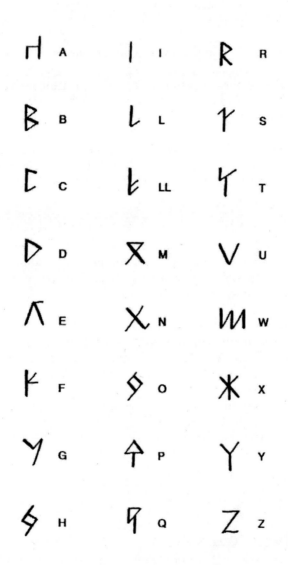

A Coelbren Alphabet - Compiled by the sixteenth century Bard,
Llewellyn Sion of Llangewydd

have used his own literary gifts, or both. Whatever the truth, the doctrine contained in 'Barddas' is strongly coloured by Qabalistic ideas, and focuses on the biblical god concept rather than on Pagan Celtic deities.

The texts relate how the three primary letters of the alphabet were shown to Menw the Aged, who saw the heavenly light as three rays and at the same time heard the divine voice - experiencing light and creative vibration as one. The discarnate voice sounded three notes, from which Menw obtained three letter sounds and their appropriate symbols. His experience also gave Menw the wisdom to assign a letter to every sound, giving rise, according to 'Barddas', to all languages.

Inspired by the three rays of light, Menw then invented the symbol for the creator's name /|\, which equates with the Tetragrammaton. This symbol, representing the Druidic Awen, spiritual illumination and inspiration, illustrates the threefold nature of existence and initiated the custom of preserving knowledge in triadic form. The three letters relating to the three strokes of the Awen symbol are OIV, or the divine name which was spoken to create the universe, and represent the sacred qualities of love, knowledge and truth.

All things vibrate to this divine name, which must not be spoken aloud, due to its sanctity and power.

Coelbren

Barddas also contains information on the bardic coelbren alphabet. It claims that the letters relate to the fundamental nature of existence, and that they were created at the same instant as the universe itself, an identical belief to that associated with the origin of the Hebrew alphabet.

In contrast to the tale of Menw, *'Barddas'* also relates how Einigan the Giant invented writing in order to inscribe a memorial to his father, Huon. As these first letters were carved on wood they were called coelbren, meaning 'the wood of credibility', 'pren' being Welsh for wood. Both the letters themselves and the pieces of wood on which they were inscribed were referred to as coelbren.

Historically, the coelbren characters possibly derive from Ogham, though they also appear to have been influenced by runes and by Roman letters. Mythologically, the sixteen letters of the first coelbren were created from the three rays of the Awen and their corresponding letters.

Tradition states that the Cymry had ten letters in their alphabet before they came from the Continent to settle in Britain, and knowledge of these early letters was closely guarded by the Bards. The sixteen letter coelbren is said to have been invented around the late fifth century BC and by the sixth century AD had been increased to eighteen letters. The Chief Bard, Taliesin, increased it yet again to twenty letters, alternatively, Ithel the Tawny was responsible for this increase in the number of characters.

Only in Taliesin's time, due to the introduction of Christianity, did OIV start to be equated with the biblical god's name.

Geraint Fardd Glas (the Blue Bard) c.900 finally enlarged the coelbren alphabet to twenty four letters, which were used both for secret writing and for divination by means of four cubic dice, ie. 6x4=24 letters. There are also Medieval versions of coelbren with thirty eight characters.

The wooden 'peithynen' frame was a 'book' for the secret writing of coelbren, employed by the early Bards. Its use was revived after the defeat of the Welsh Prince Owain Glyndwr (1349-1415), after which the English King Henry V banned writing on paper or parchment in Wales.

The Charms of the Bards

These were bars of wood called 'ebillion', about a finger long, which could be joined together to make a longer ebillion. Each small piece had part of a message or word inscribed on it, so that when they were joined together a meaning was revealed. They could be employed for secret communication by two or more initiates, or cast for divination.

Palm Coelbren

The four dice inscribed with the twenty four characters of the coelbren could be held in the palm and shown to a fellow initiate in order to spell out messages.

Coeluain

This is the term used for the bardic letters when cut on stone. 'Secret coelvains' were small stones engraved with letters, and used to form words or messages.

The Naming

Spoken words of power, sacred alphabets, storytelling and poetic inspiration .....all held an important place in Celtic life. This reverence for the word extended to a belief in the power of a person's name, which was thought to be intimately bound up with his or her character and destiny. Heroes were given a childhood name until they had 'earned' a true one, a practice which also acted as a protection against forces from the Otherworld by concealing the infant's qualities.

The sheer strength of a name is shown in *Cad Goddeu* where there is mention of a man who cannot be overcome unless his name is known. However, the magician Gwydion ap Don guesses that it is Bran.

The giving of a name was a sacred act, part of a hero's right of passage. Sometimes this naming was done by a Druid who saw the child's potential, such as in the tale of Finn MacCumhaill. At other times the naming relates to an episode which displays a person's character. After killing his host's guard dog, the hero Cuchulainn, who bore the childhood name of Setanta, takes its place until he has trained another dog, thus gaining the name of 'Culainn's hound'. He lives up to his name throughout the tales: fierce, loyal and protective, single-handedly guarding Ulster.

The Welsh myth of Llew again illustrates the importance of the name, and the tradition that it is the mother who should bestow it. Arianrhod, who gives birth to Llew whilst claiming to be a virgin, and who refuses to name him, is eventually tricked into doing so by his foster-father and uncle, Gwydion. Disguised as a shoemaker, Llew shoots a wren, leading his mother to exclaim, 'The light haired one hit it with a skilful hand.' Thus Llew (bright, shining) Llaw Gyffes (skilful hand) obtained his name.

In the Welsh myth of Pryderi it is also his mother, Rhiannon, who names him. On the night of his birth her son is stolen by a demon and believed to be dead, causing Rhiannon to suffer severe punishment for his supposed murder.

Eventually, he is brought to court by his foster father, and on being told the boy's identity Rhiannon remarks, 'What a relief from all my anxiety!', giving Pryderi his name, meaning anxiety.

The story leads up to this moment of naming, and most of the adventures are a direct cause of Pryderi's name. In a similar way, the names of places, their deities and stories, were vitally important to the early Celts.

Poetry, Myth and Place

In Ireland such stories were called 'dindsenchas', and learning them was a vital part of bardic training. Though some simply give a mythical origin for a place name, others show profound insight. Familiarity with the stories brought a deeper understanding of the land, which the Celts regarded as alive and sacred, and forged a closer bond between it and its people.

Each place can be identified by its story, in a form of code which names the legendary events which happened there rather than the actual name of the place. An example occurs in the Ulster

Cycle when the hero Cuchulainn speaks to his future wife Emer, describing the route he has just taken by a series of place myths.

In Celtic belief, natural features, such as rivers and hills or Druid groves, each had their indwelling spirit or deity. The poems and songs composed, the mythic tales told of these places, of the beings associated with them and the supernatural events that had occured there, energized the spirit of the individual place and, by extension, the entire land. It was believed that if the songs ceased to be sung or the tales to be told the vitality of the land would fade.

The role of preserving British sacred place-name stories is filled by Nennius in his work *The Seven Wonders of Britain* and by Gerald of Wales, who does the same for his own country.

Relating to a Special Place

Just as the Celts used poetry and tales to establish a closer connection to the land and to vitalize the energy of the land itself, this can still be done today.

Visit a place of special significance for you, sit and meditate there for a while, picking up on its unique spirit and beauty. Then, preferably on the spot, but otherwise later at home, write a short story or poem about the area, in whatever way seems appropriate, perhaps describing the beauty of nature and using mythological or even contemporary characters. You don't have to aim at producing a work of literary genius, or a lengthy piece, but it should come from the heart.

Having done this, do you experience an extra awareness of the place? A stronger link with it? This kind of creative writing is not meant to pin down or analyse what is intangible, but to invoke the spirit of the place by forming subtle connections.

Chapter Five

The Gift of Hermes

The Greek alphabet is the ancestor of our own, as is shown by the word itself, which is made up of the first two Greek letters, Alpha and Beta. It was adopted, and adapted, by the Romans and entered the British Isles in the form of Latin characters.

Because these characters, and in many cases the Greek, are so familiar to everyone who reads and writes English they are not easily associated with magico-religious beliefs. Yet the Greek letters possess a series of correspondences, and both alphabets are used in numerology, talismans and ritual inscriptions.

Historical Origins

The Greek root language, as distinct from the alphabet, arrived with the Hellenic tribes who came from the north and gradually settled on the mainland and islands of the Aegean after 2500 BC. The different tribes who made up the Hellenic people gave rise originally to five regional dialects, but due to the political and commercial power and the culture of Athens in the fifth century BC Attic replaced the other dialects. It was employed by dramatists such as Æschylus, Euripides and Sophocles, the philosopher Plato and the historian Herodotus. And it is the ancestor of modern Greek.

The earliest known Greek culture, the Mycenean, named after the town around which it was centred, evolved alongside the more highly advanced Minoan civizilization of Crete. During the Late Minoan period, lasting from around 1600 - 1450 BC, the two cultures were in regular contact and the Myceneans introduced the Linear B script into Crete. This was deciphered in 1953, however, the script of the Middle Minoan period, 2000 - 1600 BC, known as Linear A, remains undeciphered, as does a yet earlier hieroglyphic system.

The Mycenean culture was eventually destroyed in 1150 BC by invaders referred to by Egyptian chroniclers as 'the Sea Peoples', followed by less civilized Greek tribes from the north-west.

Then, towards the end of a 'dark age' lasting from 1200 - 800 BC, when no new art or architecture was created, Homer produced the 'Illiad' and 'Odyssey', instigating a new literary form, the epic. This had its roots in earlier ballads, transmitted orally by professional or amateur 'singers' for the entertainment of the aristocracy, as in Celtic and Teutonic culture. Many early songs about the gods and goddesses were also written down at around the same time and are referred to as 'The Homeric Hymns', though they are not now thought to be his work.

Epic literature did not involve the poet's own thoughts and feelings, he merely recorded heroic events in an impersonal manner. However, under the influence of Hesiod, author of *Works and Days* and *Theogony*, the poet also became a teacher. Knowledge of these classics followed the Greek language far from its birthplace as Alexander the Great conquered Asia Minor, Syria, Mesopotamia and Egypt in the fourth century BC.

Greek influence also played a part in many areas of Roman life, including religion, art and literature. As a new civilization they borrowed heavily from the older more established culture, in an attempt to give themselves a mythical and respectable identity.

Rome had its humble beginnings around 1000 BC when the Villanovans, a tribe of iron-working Indo-European speakers from the north-east settled in Latium, at the site which was later to become the famous city. Their meteoric rise only began after 650 BC, once they came in contact with the Etruscans, a civilized and literate people probably originating from Asia Minor, who spoke a non-Indo-European language.

10. Fragment of a disc from Crete bearing early Minoan hieroglyphs

Though the early Romans were influenced by Etruscan culture and belief, especially by their magical practices, they never used the Etruscan script, which has long since faded from use. And rather than showing a similarity to Greek or Roman letters, it is closer in form to the northern runes.

Because the Etruscans were in constant contact with Rome, when they developed trading links with the Greeks, who had colonies in southern Italy and Sicily, the first Hellenic influences reached the young city.

In the second and first centuries BC, as the Romans gradually conquered the city-states of Greece and other areas formerly under Greek rule, they absorbed yet more of Hellenic culture. This inspired the development of Latin literature, and Greek classics like the *Odyssey* were translated. Greek later became the language of the New Testament and also of a vast Byzantine literature, through its use in Constantinople and the Eastern Empire.

There is some disagreement about the historical origins of the Greek alphabet, which arrived from the Middle East, and began to be used in the second half of the eighth century BC. Scholars have always believed that the letters derived from the Phoenician alphabet which they closely resemble, and there would certainly have been contact between the ancient Greeks and Phoenician traders who travelled throughout the Mediterranean and beyond, some even settling on the islands of the archipelago.

Other more recent authorities suggest that it was the Aramaic alphabet of northern Syria that inspired the Greek, as there are similarities between it and the early Canaanite alphabet from Palestine. But there is no doubt about the Semetic origin of the letters, from whichever specific area, or about the fact that the names of the Greek letters resemble those of the Hebrew alphabet. Alpha is linked to aleph, meaning ox; beta to beth, a house; and gamma to the Hebrew gimel, meaning a camel, and so on.

Though the Greeks adopted a Semetic alphabet as their own they made two major improvements, the development of vowels and the doubling of consonants to ensure correct pronunciation, thereby making the whole process of writing more clear and precise. In the Syrian alphabet dots were used to indicate vowels, and sometimes Greek vowels were written above or below the consonant line, a sign that perhaps the two had an ancient link.

Semetic alphabets were written from right to left, but when the Greeks first began to use them they wrote back and forth, left to right, and right back to left. This was called boustrophedon, meaning to and fro like an ox ploughing a field. Only later did they change to our way of writing from left to right.

At around the same time the Ionic form of the alphabet became the standard, replacing different local variations. New letters were also adopted and older compound ones dropped, though some remained to be used as numerals.

Though in the fifth century BC all male Greek citizens were expected to be literate, and writing was a part of daily life, letters still retained an aura of mystery and sacred power.

Inventors - Human and Divine

Just as historical opinions concerning the Greek alphabet differ, there are several mythological accounts of its beginnings which may conceal factual clues. They also give an insight into how the early Greeks felt about their letters.

According to Herodotus, the Greek alphabet was invented by Cadmus, a Phoenician, showing that his account may have been inspired by history, and dramatically embelished. The legend tells how Cadmus invaded Boetia in search of his sister Europa, who had been abducted by Zeus in the shape of a bull, and there founded the city of Thebes. Herodotus said that he had personally seen an inscription in that city 'in Cadmian letters, most of them like the Ionic'.

Another account is given in the *Fables* of Caius Julius Hyginus, a Spaniard who was a friend of the poet Ovid, in which he makes several assertions. The first is that the three Fates invented the letters Alpha, Beta, Eta, Iota, Omicron, Tau and Ypsilon.

He then goes on to say that a man named Palamedes, the son of Nauplius, invented a further eleven. According to several classical writers these letters were not his only invention, the others including lighthouses, measures, scales and the disc. Besides being a scientific inventor, Palamedes was also a legendary hero on the Greek side during the Trojan war.

Hyginus says that the sixth century BC poet Simonides was responsible for Omega, Epsilon, Zeta and Psi (or Phi), a statement based on fact, as Simonides is known to have used new letters in his works, letters which later came into general use.

Finally, Hyginus claims that Epicharmus of Sicily invented Theta and Chi (or Psi and Pi). Though Epicharmus was a writer of comedies, who is thought to have edited the *Fables* and probably worked with Simonides, the Epicharmus of legend is probably one of the writer's distant ancestors bearing the same name.

Tying in with the Cadmus story, certain Greek scholars including Aristotle, believed that there were thirteen consonants in what was called the Pelasgian alphabet - equating with those invented by the Fates and Palamedes - before the Phoenician introduced three more. The Pelasgians were greatly revered, as it was said that only they remained literate after the deluge of Greek legend.

It is also Hyginus who, in an alternative explanation, states that the god Hermes was the true inventor of the alphabet, inspired by watching a group of cranes in flight. Possibly he was referring to the V-shaped formation of the whole group, which was angular like early writing cut in wood or scratched on clay.

11. Hermes/Mercury

The Greek Hermes equates with the Roman Mercury and the Egyptian Thoth, whose sacred bird was the Ibis, similar in appearance to a crane. Cranes were also sacred to the Etruscans who had a strong belief in supernatural powers. Augury, divination by the flight of birds, was a respected custom in the ancient world, and the fact that cranes were associated with the invention of the alphabet shows its mystical significance. Just as the flight of birds had to be interpreted to gain a deep understanding, so too did the letter shapes.

Hermes

Hermes was the deity who presided over travellers, eloquence, commerce, theft and trickery. With his winged sandals and cap, he not only governed travel but personified the wind, the element of air which has always been associated with the power of speech.

Greek mythology credits Hermes with the invention of the lyre, showing his control over both sound vibration and symbol. He then gave this lyre to Apollo as a peace offering after stealing the sun god's cattle. In his fable, Hyginus links the letters invented by the poet Simonides with the strings of Apollo's lyre, implying that each of the seven strings corresponded with a letter. Simonides would have had a profound understanding of such sacred correspondences as he was a Bard in a guild dedicated to the ecstatic god, Dionysus.

In return for the lyre, Apollo gave Hermes a wand or staff, the Caduceus, symbol of harmony. When it was used to pacify two fighting serpents they twined themselves around the staff, representing balanced polarity. The Caduceus also stood for Hermes' role as divine messenger, linking the realm of the gods with the world of humankind. This points to the fact that letters, when used magically, fulfil a similar function.

As the Greek god of sacred letters, Hermes was identified with the Egyptian Thoth when the two cultures came into contact and influenced each other. The name Hermes Trismegistus - Thrice

Great Hermes - refers to a legendary initiate, or perhaps to a mystery school. But it was also applied to Thoth, who ruled writing, science and magic, and the word Hermetic became synonymous with the magical arts, especially alchemy. Hermes Trismegistus was credited with inventing the widely used occult maxim 'As above, so below', again relating to the harmony between all things. *The Hermetic Canon*, a body of sacred texts, was said to have been written by Hermes Trismegistus, though it is more likely to have been compiled in the early centuries of the Christian era, by Alexandrian esotericists who based the work on ancient occult traditions.

The Muses

To the classical Greeks, creative inspiration was the gift of the nine Muses, the daughters of Jupiter and Mnemosyne, goddess of memory - essential for the singer of ballads. The poetic Muse was thought to use the poet as a vessel, into which she poured her eloquence or withheld it. He in turn poured the ballad into the ears of his listeners, and could take no personal credit for his talent.

The Muses could unite in grand inspiration and so though they ruled separate areas of learning and the arts, they were also one. By their number, nine, they are shown to be connected with the Triple Goddess of all life and death, who in many cultures was divided into the aspects of maid, mother and crone, corresponding to the three phases of the moon, new, full and waning. She is sometimes further divided into nine.

Euterpe was mistress of song, Thalia of pastoral poetry, Erato of lyric poetry, Calliope of heroic poetry and Melpomene of tragedy. Polyhymnia, who governed rhetoric, is represented holding a sceptre, symbolizing the unquestionable power of eloquence which rules the world like a monarch.

The final three Muses, not directly connected with the word, are: Clio, Muse of history, Terpsichore, who inspired dance, and Urania, Muse of astronomy and the sciences.

The Fates

The three Fates of Greek mythology, credited by Hyginus with inventing part of the alphabet, are also aspects of the threefold Goddess. The Fates, like the Goddess, both create and destroy, as does the word.

Clotho, the youngest of the Fates, the maiden aspect, starts spinning the thread of life, mingling light and dark fibres. The second Fate, Lachesis, strengthens it by twisting, and Atropos, the crone aspect, finally cuts the thread with a pair of shears.

Greek Gematria and Sacred Geometry

The metaphysical aspects of the Greek alphabet were further emphasized in the third century BC, when a system was developed linking each letter with a set of magical correspondences. And, unlike the Latin alphabet, each letter also possesses a numerical value, so they can be used in the art of Gematria.

The technique using Greek characters is fundamentally the same as that for the Hebrew alphabet, where a word is converted into a number by adding together the numerical equivalents of each letter. Initiates versed in Gematria are then able to understand secret links between various words with the same value, and to find hidden wisdom in written texts.

This was the case with the Neo-Platonists in Alexandria and the followers of Pythagoras, who, besides being a mathematician and scientist, was also a religious mystic, seeing in numbers the key to the universe. Combining his knowledge of music and number, he developed the theory that universal harmony could be found through an understanding of numerical secrets, and that all things on earth and in the realm of the gods are inextricably connected by an invisible web - the interlinking pattern symbolized by Hermes' Caduceus.

Renaissance hermeticists held similar beliefs, and the sixteenth century architect Palladio stated, 'the proportion of the voices are harmonies for the ears, those of the measurement are harmonies for the eyes.'

The sacred relationship between macrocosm and microcosm was thought to be indicated by the Golden Section, also known as the Golden Mean or Golden Proportion. This refers to the division of a line so that each part is in the same proportion to every other part, and to the whole.

The Golden Section is evident in nature, for example in the spiral of the conch shell, and the ancient Greeks believed that it existed in the dimensions of the human body, as did the classical Roman architect Vitruvius. It was most notably employed in the design of temples such as the Parthenon in Athens, and later in Renaissance cathedrals such as Chartres and in Hermetic works of art, which contain occult wisdom concealed in their very structure.

The laws of harmony found in mathematical formulae, in music and in the natural world were thought to prove the divine pattern of the creator god imprinted on his creation, and through Gematria, from which our word geometry derives, these are in turn linked to letters and words.

As Greek was the language of the New Testament, Christian Gnostic sects applied the technique of Gematria to the their scriptures, decoding esoteric messages too holy to be revealed to the general populace. Gnosis, the Greek word for knowledge, was the Christian equivalent of the Hebrew Qabalah, which itself influenced Gnostic practice, as did Pagan Greek Gematria and the 'Hermetic Canon'.

Mystics throughout the ages, both Pagan and Christian, sought hidden wisdom through a deep understanding of the Greek letters. Combined with, and linked to, the art of Gematria was the use of magical correspondences, thought to encompass all the truths of the mundane and spiritual realms.

The Correspondences of the Greek Alphabet

Alpha As the initial letter of the alphabet, Alpha represents the number 1, symbolizing new beginnings, unity, the one god of Christianity and matters of first importance. Its number in Gematria is reached by adding the letters comprising the word Alpha, which equal 532.

In Christianized Roman Britain Alpha is found inscribed in conjunction with Omega, the final letter of the alphabet, representing Christ's words in the Revelation of St John, when he says, ' I am Alpha and Omega, the beginning and the end, the first and the last'. This is reminiscent of YHVH in Hebrew belief. In both cases words and letters are linked to the fundamental concepts of creation, the beginning and the ending and all that lies in between. This letter symbol occurs on artefacts such as lead tanks, which were probably used for baptism.

The meaning of Alpha is cattle, representing wealth. However, this does not refer simply to abundance on the physical plane but also to spiritual riches. The possession of cattle, by which wealth and status were judged, was of prime concern at the time the alphabet was compiled, hence its positioning as the first letter, not only in the Greek but in both the Hebrew and Runic alphabets.

To the Gnostics Alpha represented the first of the seven heavens.

Beta Numerical value 2. Value in Gematria 308.

Two is associated with duality, the one dividing, finding its opposite polarity. In religions such as Christianity this opposite is regarded as evil, God versus the Devil. But two separate things possess a relationship. Whereas complete unity is static, imbalance creates change to break the state of inertia, and when there are two there is also the opportunity for reunion.

A α Alpha 1	I ι Iota 10	P ρ Rho 100
B β Beta 2	K κ Kappa 20	Σ σ Sigma 200
Γ γ Gamma 3	Λ λ Lambda 30	T τ Tau 300
Δ δ Delta 4	M μ Mu 40	Υ υ Ypsilon 400
E ε Epsilon 5	N ν Nu 50	Φ φ Phi 500
Z ζ Zeta 7	Ξ ξ Xei 60	X χ Chi 600
H η Eta 8	O ο Omicron 70	Ψ ψ Psi 700
Θ θ Theta 9	Π π Pi 80	Ω ω Omega 800

The Greek Alphabet - Giving the numerical values of the letters

Gamma Numerical value 3. Value in Gematria 85.

Three is a universally sacred number, found in many Pagan pantheons, giving Gamma the meaning of divinity. Two separate polarities are united to produce a third, as with the Egyptian Isis and Osiris and their son Horus. The Goddess too has her aspects of maid, mother and crone, symbolizing birth, growth and death, which in turn leads to rebirth on the ever turning wheel of life. Similar in concept are the three Fates. In Christianity the Holy Trinity of Father, Son and Holy Ghost again reflects the divine nature of this number.

Delta Numerical value 4. Value in Gematria 340.

Delta stands for all which is of a fourfold nature, for example the elements of fire, water, air and earth, the four seasons and the cardinal points of the compass. In the four sides of a square or the four walls of a building, this number symbolizes stability and completion.

Epsilon Numerical value 5. Value in Gematria 445.

This letter represents the fifth, unseen, element of spirit or ether, the Greek 'pneuma' or breath of life.

Epsilon plays an important role in sacred geometry due to its connection with the Golden Section. If a pentagram is drawn within a pentagon, ie. a regular five-sided figure, the relationship of the lines of the former to the latter will have the ratio of the Golden Section.

For the Gnostic Christians Epsilon symbolized the second heaven.

Zeta Though this is the sixth letter of the alphabet, it represents the number 7, due to the original sixth letter, Digamma - F, being dropped, except for mathamatical purposes. Zeta's value in Gematria is 316.

The sixth letter is associated with creation as, according to the Bible, the world was created in six days, followed by a seventh of rest.

Eta the seventh letter of the alphabet, though its numerical value is 8, the solar number. In Gematria its letters add up to 309, the number of Ares, Greek god of war.

Like three, seven is a potent esoteric number, associated with the seven days of the w eek and the seven planets of early astronomy, and also with the seven heavens of the Gnostic Christians. Because of this, Eta shares in the harmonious and balanced nature of the cosmos.

To the Christians Eta represented salvation, and was linked with their third heaven.

Theta Th is the eighth letter in the alphabet, but represents 9 numerically, and therefore has associations with both numbers. In Gematria its value is 318, equivalent to that of the sun god Helios.

Theta is linked with the crystal sphere, the eighth cosmic sphere, which was believed to support the fixed stars. As such, it represents balance. And, as the symbol for the number nine, Theta is associated with the moon, mystically linking it with the sun.

Iota Numerical value 10. In Gematria it equals 381, which is also the number of Aeolus, god of the winds. Iota is sacred to Ananke, goddess of fate, and also to the three Fates, who are said to have created it. Iota occurs as a modern figure of speech, as in when someone does not 'care an iota', indicating that the letter is small and unimportant. However, as it is the letter of fate this idea can be deceptive, and what seems trivial can have great significance.

To the Gnostics Iota was representative of the fourth heaven.

Kappa Numerical value 20. Value in Gematria 182. Kappa is the letter of misfortune, connected with illness, old age and death. The two latter are associated with the passage of time, ruled by the god Kronos, to which Kappa is sacred.

Lambda Numerical value 30. Value in Gematria 78. Lambda is of great importance in sacred geometry, as it is linked with the Golden Section. In shape it resembles the geometric tool used for creating this, which is still familiar as the symbol of Freemasonry. Lambda also represents both plant growth and spiritual ascent.

Mu Numerical value 40. Value in Gematria 440. Mu is the letter of stability and security, associated with trees which are known for their sturdy longevity. As the cosmic tree symbolically unites all three levels of existence, the Underworld, the world of men and that of the gods, likewise Mu stands for unity.

Nu Numerical value 50. Value in Gematria 450. As the thirteenth letter of the alphabet, Nu is associated with Hecate, Greek goddess of the Underworld. She is the crone aspect of the Triple Goddess, and lady of the dark moon. But though she rules death, it is followed by rebirth, just as the new moon appears after a period of darkness.

Xei Numerical value 60. Value in Gematria 615. Xei is the fourteenth letter of the alphabet, and represented the fifteen fixed stars of ancient belief. In Medieval magic these were given magical sigils and were used in the construction of talismans.

Omicron Numerical value 70. Value in Gematria 1090. As its shape indicates, Omicron is associated with the sun, and the solar deities Apollo and Helios. It also has connections with Christ, as the son of light.

For the Gnostics this letter represented the fifth heaven.

ᚠ	F	FEOH	Wealth	ᛋ	S	SIGEL	Sun
ᚢ	U	UR	Aurochs	↑	T	TIR	Tyr
ᚦ	Th	ThORN	Thorn	ᛒ	B	BEORC	Birch
ᚩ	O	OS	God/Mouth	ᛖ	E	EH	Horse
ᚱ	R	RAD	Riding	ᛗ	M	MAN	Man
ᚳ	C	CEN	Torch	ᛚ	L	LAGU	Ocean
ᚷ	G	GYFU	Gift	ᛝ	Ng	ING	Ing
ᚹ	W	WENNE	Bliss	ᛞ	D	DAEG	Day
ᚻ	H	HAEGL	Hail	ᛟ	E	EThEL	Estate
ᚾ	N	NYD	Need	ᚪ	A	AC	Oak
ᛁ	I	IS	Ice	ᚨ	AE	AESC	Ash
ᛄ	J	GER	Year	ᚤ	Y	YR	Bow?
ᛇ	Y	EOH	Yew	ᛡ	IO	IAR	Otter?
ᛈ	P	PEORD	Chessman	ᛠ	EA	EAR	Grave?
ᛉ	Z	EOLH	Sedge				

The Etruscan Alphabet

Pi Numerical value 80. Number in Gematria 101. Like Omicron, Pi is associated with the sun, but it also has links with the sun's sixteen symbolic rays. These stand for the divine illumination of solar deities such as Apollo and Christ, and are depicted in Medieval Christian art.

Rho Numerical value 100. Number in Gematria 170. As the seventeenth letter of the alphabet Rho represents fruitfulness and fertility. It also figures in the Christianized Roman Chi-Rho symbol ☧ , which uses the first two letters of the Greek word Christos. An example is shown on the mosaic floor of a Roman villa at Hinton St Mary, Dorset, where the symbol is depicted behind the head of a figure representing Christ. It is sometimes found in association with the Alpha - Omega symbol.

Sigma Numerical value 200. Value in Gematria 254. Sigma is associated in ancient Greek belief with Hermes as the guide of dead souls to Hades.

Tau Numerical value 300. Value in Gematria 701. The shape of the letter Tau is a pictogram for man, the microcosm. It is identical to the lower section of the Egyptian ankh, symbol of eternal life, from which it may derive. For Christians the Tau represents the cross on which Jesus died, as historically this was the shape of crosses used for crucifixion. Tau also symbolizes the Christian Trinity.

Ypsilon Numerical value 400. Value in Gematria 1260. This character stands for the element of water in Greek belief, and everything which shares its flowing nature. For the Gnostics Ypsilon was associated with the sixth heaven.

Phi Numerical value 500. Value in Gematria 510. Phi is symbolic of the phallus, and masculine creative energy. It is also associated with the Greek god Pan, meaning 'all', the unity behind all existence. This letter is used as the symbol for the Golden Section.

12. Chi-Rho symbol incorporated into a design from the Roman
villa at Hinton St Mary, Dorset. The figure almost certainly
depicts Christ as the symbol lies behind his head and is flanked
by pomegranates, associated with eternal life.

Chi Ch Numerical value 600. Value in Gematria 610. Chi symbolizes property and possessions. It is also associated, through gematria, with the cosmos, Greek 'kosmos', the letters of which add to 600.

Psi Ps Numerical value 700. Value in Gematria 710. Psi is a letter of illumination, linked to Zeus, father of the Greek gods, as the embodiment of celestial light. It is also associated, on the mundane level, with daylight. The letters in the Christian symbol Chi-Rho add to 700 by Gematria, linking psi to Christ as the son of light.

Omega Numerical value 800. Value by Gematria 849. As the final letter of the alphabet Omega is symbolic of conclusion. It is also associated with wealth and plenty, reminiscent of Alpha. Omega is linked with the Greek word pistis, meaning faith, and kyrios, meaning lord, which both have the number 800 in gematria, and can be applied to either Pagan or Christian belief.

In Gnostic doctrine Omega represents the seventh heaven.

Numerology

Modern numerology using the Latin alphabet is similar in many ways to Greek Gematria, though now the technique is most commonly used for gaining an insight into a person's character and/or direction in life. This is done by calculating the numerical equivalent of the subject's full name, his or her formal name (ie. the name used when signing business documents), or simply the first name or nickname.

The full name gives a general outline of character and ambition, the formal name governs business and social affairs, while the first name or nickname is associated with everyday life. Numerologists believe that a certain amount can also be learnt from the initial letter of a name, which is the first expression of the subject's character.

A person's name is considered to be of great significance in many cultures, affecting both earthly health and well-being and even the survival of the spirit after death. Modern numerology also subscribes to the theory that character and destiny are inextricably bound up with the name.

A table for discovering the numerical values of the letters is referred to by numerologists as a systemata. The most common one, known as the *Pythagorean systemata*, is as follows:

1	2	3	4	5	6	7	8	9
A	B	C	D	E	F	G	H	I
J	K	L	M	N	O	P	Q	R
S	T	U	V	W	X	Y	Z	

The name is reduced to a single number between 1 and 9, which is then associated with the qualities of one of the planets. For example JANE WHITE = 1+1+5+5 +5+8+9+2+5 = 41, then 4+1= 5, making her a number 5 person with the characteristics of a Mercurian type. The astrological attributions are as follows:

1 - Sun	4 - Uranus	7 - Neptune
2 - Moon	5 - Mercury	8 - Saturn
3 - Jupiter	6 - Venus	9 - Mars

Character analysis is never simple or one-dimensional, but the following is a brief outline of the basic personality traits of each numerological type.

1 - The Sun - Number ones are self-starters with a great deal of energy and ambition. They are extrovert, dealing with the outer world rather than searching within. People ruled by the sun will be full of creative ideas but can also be egotistical, thinking that the whole world revolves around them.

2 - The Moon - Lunar people are often concerned with the inner realms, with psychic powers, imagination and intuition. They are also drawn to nurturing and homemaking as they love children and the family environment. With their caring attitude, number twos make good teachers, nurses and social workers. The Moon with her rhythms can make number two people moody and changeable, showing different faces at different times. They can also lack self-confidence, or be over-sensitive.

3 - Jupiter - Number 3 people are outgoing, cheerful, confident and trustworthy. They have large-scale ambitions, and are conscientious about achieving them. As lovers of order and discipline, they do well in positions of authority, especially in the services or in government posts. On the negative side, they can be domineering and arrogant.

4 - Uranus - Uranian people are highly individual, sometimes even eccentric, the rebels of the world. They are natural inventors and scientists and are also concerned with humanitarian issues, though they can appear distant on a personal level. Number fours have to guard against being too highly strung and sensitive.

5 - Mercury - As Mercury is the planet, and deity, of communication, number fives excel in this area, as good writers, conversationalists and teachers. They also enjoy travel and learning but can be flighty, veering from one direction to another, never exploring any subject in great depth. This characteristic does, however, give them great resiliance as they do not dwell on problems. Though Mercurians are sociable, they also tend to be nervous and over-excitable.

6 - Venus - People ruled by number six are idealists with a romantic attitude to life. They are friendly and affectionate, and hate any form of disharmony. Sixes love art and beautiful objects, and seek the sensual pleasures of life.

7 - Neptune - Sevens are the mystics of the world, often possessing a magnetic quality which draws others to them. Due to their inspirational nature, besides being psychics and clairvoyants, they do well as artists and poets. Those ruled by number seven can be restless, loving change and travel, especially that associated with the sea. They also tend to be unrealistic dreamers who have little time for material concerns.

8 - Saturn - Number eights are serious, and steady hard workers whose determination leads to eventual success. They do best in positions requiring responsibility. These people are not gregarious and do not make friends easily, which might lead to loneliness in life. They are also likely to be over-conventional and cautious.

9 - Mars - People ruled by number nine are energetic and active. They can also be hot-tempered, or impulsive and foolhardy, which often causes strife. Number nines are courageous, and do best to use their energy and competitiveness in sport, or as leaders of a cause.

The birth date can also be reduced to a single digit to give an insight into a person's character and the lessons to be learnt in life. This digit is referred to as the destiny number. For a fuller picture, the attributions of the birthday, the birth month and the year can be separately analyzed. The day relates to everyday life, the month to business and social life, and the year to the spiritual lessons that must be learnt in order to evolve. All the numbers can be referred to the planetary qualities listed above.

There are several systemata used in numerology for discovering name and birthdate values. Once these are calculated, the processes involved in interpreting a full numerological chart are very detailed, analyzing each name number, then relating it to the other name numbers, and to the destiny number. Both name and destiny numbers can be further related to a specific date to see if that day will be fortunate. Each number has a positive or negative aspect to the others, which must also be taken into consideration when making a reading.

As there are many books on numerology, covering the subject in depth, the above is only a taster. It would be impossible to do justice to the art of either numerology or astrology in a few paragraphs, so please refer to the bibliography for further information.

Inscriptions, Supplications and Curses

The written word always played an important role in Roman civilization, usually for mundane purposes such as official records, but letters were also used in magical and religious contexts. If special emphasis was needed, for example when appealing to a god for prosperity or to harm an enemy, simply speaking the request was not deemed sufficient. Artefacts illustrating this belief have been found in all areas of the Empire, including Britain.

After the conquest, the Romans linked their deities to those of the native Britons, who also adopted some Roman occult practices. One such practice was the writing of curses on lead tablets, which were then rolled up so that only the god appealed to for help would be aware of the contents, and in some cases the tablets were nailed to the temple wall. The fact that the curse had to be written meant that greater concentration and mental clarity was required, similar to the process of making a talisman. Magical intent was focused into the lead tablet as the ill-wisher wrote, and the nail was driven through it to activate the spell.

At the temple of Uley in Gloucestershire, which was dedicated to Mercury, over two hundred lead tablets have been found. The Romano-Celtic temple at Bath, Somerset,also yielded a large number, detailing the sufferings and unpleasant deaths wished upon theives, rapists, murderers and unfaithful lovers. Besides cursing tablets, votive plaques made of bronze or silver were engraved in the hope of securing a god's favour. Stone altars bearing dedications to Roman or native gods or to local spirits are also known, the lettering usually carved in formal capitals as opposed to the cursive script which was used for everyday purposes.

At Bath an altar inscription addressed to Sul, goddess of the springs, ends with LM, libens merito, an abreviation for a phrase meaning 'the votary fulfils cheerfully the vow which he acknowledges as due for mercies rendered'.

Word squares were also employed for magical purposes, for example:

ROTAS

OPERA

TENET

AREPO

SATOR

Translated as 'The sower Arepo guides the wheels carefully', the above was supposed to guard against disease and death by fire. An early example was found in the ruins of Pompeii.

It was later used as a Christian cryptogram for embodying a sacred truth, linking Pater Noster (Our Father) with AO (Alpha Omega):

```
            A
            P
            A
            T
            E
            R
A/PATERNOSTER/O
            O
            S
            T
            E
            R
            O
```

Word squares, including the SATOR square, also played a major part in Medieval occultism, though its main influence was Qabalistic.

Letters and Magic

In modern esoteric work our own Latin alphabet is every bit as valid as more ancient or obscure sacred alphabets.

One of its chief uses is in the creation of talismans where letters, symbols, or a combination of both, synthesizing the nature of what is required, are written on a piece of paper and consecrated, for beneficial purposes only. The Romano-British practice of making cursing tablets is not to be recommended! Besides being unethical, ill-wishing eventually rebounds on the sender.

Certain rituals perfromed today require that the aim of the rite is written on a piece of paper, used in conjunction with the appropriate herbs, candles, symbols, visualization and spoken words. Then paper is burnt, the request placed in the hands of the gods to bring about its fruition.

In candle magic the purpose of the work can be inscribed on a candle, as briefly as possible. In all cases the wording requires focus and a clear expression of purpose. The ritual intent is concentrated in the words, and emotions are poured through them.

Also useful in magical work, is the system of colour correspondences attributed to the letters of the Latin alphabet:

A, I, J, Q and Y - orange, tawny and rich brown

B, C, K and R - white

G, L and S - scarlet

D, M and T - purple and violet

E and N - blue-grey

U, V, W and X - light blue

O and Z - green

F, H and P - dark blue

There are infinite creative and magical possibilities offered by the Greek and Latin alphabets, even though they are living alphabets used in the mundane world.

Chapter Six

Runic Wisdom

According to Norse mythology, the runes were obtained through self-sacrifice by the god Odin, showing how all inspiration and wisdom demands its price. As the product of divine illumination they were credited with powerful magical properties and had uses in many areas of life, from shamanic initiation to protection in battle. They were also later employed for mundane purposes, such as business records and personal messages.

But, despite the importance of the runes, the early northern tradition, like that of the Celts, was an oral one in which history and myth were transmitted from one generation to the next by word of mouth.

Though our modern alphabet is Latin, not runic, and many of our words also derive from the Roman tongue, English means the language of the Angles, a people who spoke one of the West Germanic dialects.

Historical Background

The original homeland of the Teutonic peoples who settled the north is unknown, but they began to leave these homelands in search of new pastures around 2500 BC, and during the last centures BC colonized the south of the Scandinavian peninsula, the Baltic Islands and northern Germany. Despite their success in conquest, and the fact that they shared a common language and a similar culture, the many tribes never united as one nation. Again like the Celts, they remained independent and were frequently at war with each other.

Due to lack of written records nothing is known of the early days of these peoples, but in the historical era they were divided into three major branches: the Goths in eastern Europe, the Teutons who settled in Scandinavia, and the West Germans, the ancestors of the Angles and Saxons. Throughout this chapter I use the word 'Teutonic' to describe the people from all three branches, not simply with reference to the Scandinavians.

In the fifth century AD numerous Teutonic tribes swept across the western Roman Empire, fleeing from the Huns, and caused the Romans to withdraw from Britain in order to protect their Continental interests. After this withdrawal Angles, Saxons, Jutes, Danes and Norwegians invaded, and finally settled in the British Isles.

Then, in the tenth century AD a number of Norwegian chieftans again left their native shores due to the policies of Harald Fairhair, and set sail for Iceland where they settled, preserving the ancient traditions of their land. Modern Icelandic is very similar to Old Norse, which has aided the understanding of runic inscriptions and the translation of Old Norse manuscripts.

The only surviving written material in the Gothic language is Biblical translation and commentary, composed after many of the Goths were converted to Christianity in the fourth century as a result of their contact with the Byzantine civilization. Few West Germanic myths have survived either, though Ceasar and Tacitus did comment on them, equating the northern gods with those of the Romans. The Germanic monks and clerks who were the first to write in their own language scarcely mention the religions of the people they sought to convert. Only popular tales, handed down for generations by word of mouth, preserved some of the early beliefs.

Most of the ancient Teutonic myths known today come from the Scandinavian tradition, as this alone was set down in writing. In Denmark, Sweden, Norway and Iceland Medieval writers recorded ancient songs, sagas, poetry and historical accounts before they were irretrievably lost. The Icelandic records are particularly detailed and illuminating, and because of the country's late conversion to Christianity, in the early eleventh century, one section of the collection of poems known as the Eddas was composed while Paganism still flourished.

Language

Like Greek, Latin and Celtic, the Teutonic languages are of the Indo-European family, though there are several dialects, ancient and modern. Old Norse, Gothic, Old High German, Old English and Old Saxon are the forerunners of the Scandinavian languages, Icelandic, German and English, though in the latter case there is a strong Latin influence.

Historical Origins of the Runes

Runes in their various forms were the earliest letter symbols employed for writing these languages. As with other alphabets, there is uncertainty over the roots of the letters, with the result that several theories have been put forward in the nineteenth and twentieth centuries.

Some scholars believe that the northern tribes developed their 'alphabets' after coming in contact with Roman civilization in the second century BC, basing their own letters on the Latin characters. The use of runes would then have spread north along the early trade routes to Scandinavia.

The second theory is that the runes were developed by the Goths, inspired by the Greek cursive script. This is now disregarded by most experts because the Goths did not come into contact with Greek culture until around 200 AD, by which time the runes were already in existence.

Thirdly, there are close similarities between the earliest forms of the runic characters and those of the Etruscan or North Italic alphabet. As the Etruscans travelled to northern Europe to trade for amber, their alphabet would have become familiar to the tribes they had dealings with, who could easily have adopted the

The Hällristningar Cult Symbols

script for their own use. The Teutonic peoples of the Alps would also have been in contact with the Etruscans around 300 BC, though this predates the earliest runic evidence by three or four hundred years. An inscription on the Negau helmet from the border between Austria and the former Yugoslavia, dating to c.300 BC, is in the Teutonic language but uses Etruscan characters.

Though the Etruscan alphabet has been deciphered, the meanings of the letters are unknown, so they cannot be given a magical interpretation which might link them more closely with the runes.

The final theory claims that the runes were invented in the Teutonic homelands themselves, based on ancient ideographs. The early Teutons did use ideographs, such as the Hällristningar, found on Neolithic and Bronze Age rock carvings, but they do not appear to have been alphabetical, discrediting this theory. However, it is very likely that ideographs influenced some of the letter shapes developed from the alphabets of other cultures and also gave the letters their names and esoteric meanings.

History of the Runes

The word 'rune' derives from an Indo-European root 'ru' meaning either mystery or to whisper, the latter associating it with the power of voice vibration used in incantations. In all the Teutonic languages words employing this root have the meaning of mystery or secret, for example Old Norse and Old English 'rûn'; Gothic, Old High German and Old Saxon 'rúna'.

The characters would originally have been carved in stone or wood, which accounts for their angular shapes, though the oldest known runic inscription is engraved on the Meldorf brooch from Jutland, Denmark, which dates to around 50 AD. Due to this early method of writing in the north, the Old German word 'wrítu', meaning 'I carve', has given rise to our modern word 'write'. Another etymological association between wood and

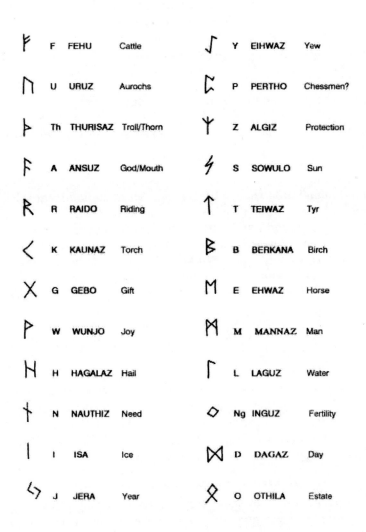

	F	FEHU	Cattle		Y	EIHWAZ	Yew
	U	URUZ	Aurochs		P	PERTHO	Chessmen?
	Th	THURISAZ	Troll/Thorn		Z	ALGIZ	Protection
	A	ANSUZ	God/Mouth		S	SOWULO	Sun
	R	RAIDO	Riding		T	TEIWAZ	Tyr
	K	KAUNAZ	Torch		B	BERKANA	Birch
	G	GEBO	Gift		E	EHWAZ	Horse
	W	WUNJO	Joy		M	MANNAZ	Man
	H	HAGALAZ	Hail		L	LAGUZ	Water
	N	NAUTHIZ	Need		Ng	INGUZ	Fertility
	I	ISA	Ice		D	DAGAZ	Day
	J	JERA	Year		O	OTHILA	Estate

The Elder Futhark

letters occurs in the word 'stave', or stick. This came to mean a rune, indicating that originally the characters were carved on small pieces of wood which could be used for divination, as in the Celtic tradition.

There are three major rune systems: the Elder Futhark (or Common Germanic Futhark), the Anglo-Saxon Futhork and the Viking (or Younger) Futhork, which was developed in Scandinavia. The name Futhark or Futhork relates to the order of the letters in the same way as the name for the Latin 'alphabet' derives from alpha and beta, the first two letters of the Greek system on which it was based.

The Elder Futhark was employed from the earliest times until about 800 AD. It was arranged in a precise order and consisted of twenty-four characters, each with a name. There are only about three hundred Elder Futhark inscriptions in existence, as most runes would have been carved on perishable materials such as wood and bone which have not survived.

From the seventh century AD new variants began to evolve from the Elder Futhark, and by 800 AD had succeeded it, though the Elder system continued to be used in secret magical traditions.

The Anglo-Saxon Futhork was developed in England and consisted of twenty-eight, twenty-nine or thirty-three symbols. The second derivative was the Viking Futhork, found in Viking Scandinavia, in which the original system was reduced to sixteen characters. Rune poems give us the symbolic meanings of the Anglo-Saxon and Viking Furthorks, but unfortunately none exist for the Elder Furthark.

During the period when the Teutonic lands were being converted to Christianity the old beliefs and the new continued side by side for some time. Runes were often employed as a mystical alphabet for the new faith, for example the Ruthwell Cross in Dumfries bears a runic inscription telling the story of the crucifixion, and combines Pagan symbols with Christian scenes. Another example is the Franks Casket, believed to have been made in Northumbria in the early eighth century, which also depicts both biblical and Pagan scenes, explained in runic characters.

In Denmark, at the end of the tenth century a system of dotted runes was developed to assist understanding. And in the thirteenth century the first runic alphabet was created, alotting a rune symbol to each of the Latin characters.

By this date much of the esoteric lore and symbolism associated with the runes had been lost and they were increasingly being put to mundane uses. In the thirteenth and fourteenth centuries they were employed for writing messages, such as the note found in Bergen, Norway, from a woman to her husband, asking him to come home from the inn! In addition, they were used for almanacs and merchants' tallies.

Also around this time, writing with pen and ink was replacing the traditional carving method. The manuscripts in which the rune poems are recorded are particularly important as they give a wealth of information about the letter meanings.

Despite the fact that in most areas the esoteric understanding of runes was gradually lost and the letters replaced by Latin characters, folk tradition preserved some of the ancient knowledge. In remote parts of Scandinavia, chiefly Sweden, and Iceland, runes continued to be used for writing in the twentieth century, though from the mid-eighteenth century the symbols were combined with Latin characters. Rune-lore also continued to be practised; magical rune-singers existed in areas of the Scandinavian peninsula, and in Iceland the magical employment of runes survived into the seventeenth century.

Poetry, Myth and Saga

The main source of our knowledge about Teutonic myth and religious belief is the Norse literature of Iceland, based on the traditions of those who settled there to escape persecution in their native Norway. A great deal of this ancient Pagan poetry was collected in the late thirteenth century by a Christian priest named Sæmund, and is known as the Elder or Poetic Edda. Its subject matter is either heroic, sometimes based on histoircal events, or mythological. The poetry was originally composed during different periods, some of the heroic lays probably dating from as early as the eighth century, while other material was written in Iceland betwen the eleventh and thirteenth centuries.

The 'Völupsá' (Sibyl's Prophecy) tells the tale of the world, the acts of the gods and of humans from the creation to Ragnarök (the fall of the gods). It is thought that it was written at the end of the Pagan era and was probably influenced by Christian belief of the kind found in the 'Revelation of St John'.

The above poem is followed by the 'Hávamál' (Words of the High One), supposedly given by Odin. A section of this, entitled 'Runatál', describes his self-sacrifice in order to obtain the runes, and also his instructions in rune-craft.

Norse literature is also found in the form of sagas, first written down in the late twelfth century but probably deriving from earlier oral tales. They deal with several subject matters, the most important being the kings of Norway, Icelandic settlers, hero tales and mythology.

The best known of the saga writers is Snorri Sturluson (1179-1241), author of *Heimskringla*, a history of the Norwegian kings spanning several centuries. It is thought that Snorri also wrote the saga of Egil Skallagrimsson, a tenth century runemaster, Skald and adventurer. His other famous work is *The Younger Edda* in which he deals with the language and style of early Norse poetry.

The Skalds

In the ancient Scandinavian tradition the Skalds were equivalent to the Celtic Bards, the composers and reciters of poetry which followed established technical patterns. Skaldic poetry contained fantastic imagery and the words were often

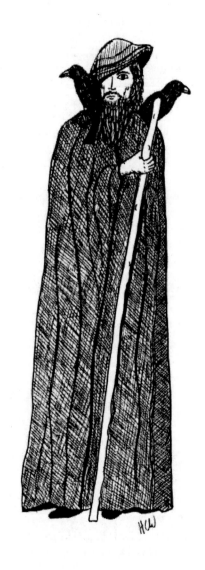

13. 'Grim'

placed in an unnatural order, these factors combining to make the work very complex. Many skaldic poems were written in praise of their noble masters, and were descriptive rather than narrative.

As it differs greatly from Germanic tradition, the skaldic art is believed to have developed independently in nineth century Norway, where it originated, before continuing in Iceland, the birthplace of the renowned poet, Egil Skallagrimsson (c.910 - 90). Through his exploits, Norse literature shows us the connection between the skaldic art and that of the runemaster, a skill he was also adept in. In addition, Egil was a widely travelled man, who composed much of his literary work in Norway and England.

Mythical Origins of the Runes

Odin - Shaman and Runemaster

In Norse mythology the patron of both Skalds and runemasters was the chief god Odin (Old High German - Wuotan/ Old English - Woden) who bore the title Allfather, indicating his prime position and multiple roles. He presided over war and warriors, statesmen, and the dead. He was also divine runemaster, shaman, lord of magic and possessor of ultimate wisdom.

Odin's name is thought to derive from the Old Norse root 'od', meaning 'wind' or 'spirit', hence linking him to the divine spirit of poetic inspiration, similar to the druidic Awen. The ending 'in' has the meaning 'master of'. Many deities of storm and wind are associated with the sacred word, the expressive breath. As a storm god, Odin was believed to ride at the head of the Wild Hunt on his eight-legged stallion Sleipnir, seeking souls as he and his train swept across the sky amidst racing clouds.

Odin was visualized as a tall lean muscular man, either with dark hair or a bald head and long grey beard. In his own realm or when joining in battle he wore the helmet and armour of a warrior, but when mingling peacefully with men his form was usually concealed by a long mantle and a wide-brimmed hat, pulled low to hide the socket of his missing eye. From the latter guise Odin was given the title 'grim', meaning 'hooded' or 'masked', his appearance symbolizing his hidden aspect. As a shaman he was also capable of assuming any form at will.

Two ravens, Hugin (thought or mind) and Munin (memory), perched on Odin's shoulders, symbolizing his mastery over wisdom and the poetic arts.

In his quest for wisdom, Odin's first act was to seek a draught from the Well of Mimir (memory), which could bestow the gift of fore-knowledge, and which was guarded by the oracular head of the giant, Mimir.

When the two 'families' of Norse gods, the Vanir and the Æsir, of whom Odin was chief, initially made peace they exchanged hostages, including Mimir. But the Vanir beheaded the giant in anger on discovering that another hostage, Hœnir, only lived up to his wise reputation when advised by Mimir. When the head was returned to the Æsir, Odin preserved it with herbs and kept it alive by spell-working.

Mimir's head would only permit Odin to drink from the well, the source of memory, if the god was willing to sacrifice one of his eyes. Despite the magnitude of this demand Odin agreed, putting his quest before all else. He sunk his eye into the depths of the well, giving him a permanent connection with the realms of the subconscious, the deep primal waters. He then took a long draught, thus obtaining wisdom and the power to see into the future, including the ultimate fall of the gods, Ragnarök.

To mark his sacrifice and its reward Odin took a branch from the World Tree, Yggdrasil, and created his spear, Gungnir, from it. According to the 'Runatál', Odin again made a sacrifice in order to gain runic wisdom, impaling himself with this spear on the World Tree from which it was fashioned:

'I know I hung on the wind-swept tree,
Its roots to the wise unknown;
Spear-pierced, for nine long nights,
To Odin pledged, self offered to self,

They gave no bread, nor drinking horn;
Down into the depths I gazed:
Crying aloud I took up the runes,
Then finally I fell.'

In the Norse tradition, Yggdrasil, usually symbolized by an ash tree, represents the created world and all levels of existence, with Asgard, the realm of the gods, at the summit, Midgard, the world of men, in the centre and below, the frozen kingdom of Hel, where the souls of those who died of disease or old age, a 'straw death', were relegated.

Odin's ordeal lasted for nine nights, symbolizing the lunar gift of inspiration offered by the Triple Goddess, or by the three Norns, the power of their sacred number magnified through multiplication by itself. At the end of this time Odin cried out, and grabbing the runes he fell from the tree.

The symbolism of his sacrifice describes Odin's runic initiation as a shaman journeying between worlds. The runes, too, are a bridge between worlds, symbols on the material plane evoking deeper esoteric meanings. Odin descended into the realm of the dead, the unconscious, the domain of the Dark Mother, where he received inspiration that could be taught to mankind to broaden consciousness.

It is interesting that in the 'Runatál' Odin says he sacrificed himself to himself, working on his own inner self to achieve illumination. He attained integration, union of the higher and lower selves, becoming whole through the all-pervading inspiration of the runes, which reach every level of being.

As he obtained the runes Odin cried out, emphasizing the transformational power of vibration, of vocalized sound, the breath that transforms the inaminate into the living, the mundane into the inspired.

At the conclusion of his ordeal Odin carved runes on many objects including the teeth of Sleipnir, the claws of the bear and on the shaft of Gungnir. These upheld the power of the law, so that any oath sworn upon the spear's point could not be broken.

In the Norse creation myth, Odin was one of a triad of creator gods, Odin, Vili and Vé, all three being aspects of himself. As mentioned above, Odin's name is associated with spirit, Vili has the meaning of the will and Vé of holy - the mystery of the sacred.

These three aspects of the Allfather created the earth from the body parts of the primal giant, Ymir. They then created the first man from an ash tree, Ask, and the first woman from an elm, Embla. Odin gave them spirit or life-breath, Vili mental ability, and Vé human form, the power of speech and the senses.

Though Odin does not obviously create mankind by the power of the word, this is in fact his prime mythological function. He gives spirit/the breath of life to the first humans, and by extension to all humankind. In many traditions this is linked to, or identical with, the creative word, and Odin's fourth gift, the integrated wisdom of the runes, reveals the connection between symbol and sound and all things in creation, which are imbued with divine inspiration.

As lord of battle Odin is also a part of the breaking down process, which culminates in his gathering of souls. In a similar way, his gift of the runes can be used to build up or to break down - creating and destroying. On a mundane level the element of air associated with his name gives us life, whereas the winds of the hurricane destroy. The power of the word is borne on the breath, as eternal life is borne by the spirit.

Some authorities suggest that Odin may have been a living person, who came to be worshipped as a god after his death. If this is the case it is possible that he was a tribal shaman who underwent a symbolic ritual sacrifice involving self-wounding - a recognized part of shamanic practice found in the American Indian tradition, using pain to open the body's psychic centres. As a result, Odin 'received' a magical alphabet whilst in trance.

Linked to Odin's achievement of wisdom and his runic initiation was his quest to obtain the mead of poetic inspiration. At the time when hostages were exchanged by the Æsir and Vanir, as a sign of their truce, the two sides also spat into a cauldron and from this spittle a wise being named Kvasir was created, a being who had the abilty to answer any question.

Because of this reputation, Kvasir was killed by two dwarves who coverted his gift. They poured his blood into three vessels: Odhroerir (inspiration) - also the name of the mead - Son (expiation) and Boden (container). They then blended the blood with honey, thus making a brew which had the power to bestow poetic inspiration.

This later came into the possession of a giant named Suttung, who gave it to his daughter, Gunlod, to guard in the depths of a mountain. Assuming the form of a serpent, Odin managed to enter the mountain and, after sleeping three nights with Gunlod consumed all the mead and flew back to the Æsir in the form of an eagle. Upon reaching his own realm he spat out the mead, however, on his journey he had lost one drop, which came to be known as the poet's share.

Again, this myth takes the form of an Underworld intiation, with Odin descending into the depths of the mountain, into the womb of the Dark Mother, for three nights, a lunar number connected to the nine nights he hung on the World Tree. There, he gains the power of poetic inspiration for the gods, a drop of which is bestowed on human poets or Skalds.

The Power of Poetry

It is impossible to separate the use of runes for magical purposes from the power of magical verse, as most charms and incantations intoned over runic talismans were in verse. Odin, lord of the runes, also possessed the gift of poetic inspiration.

Teutonic magicians believed that the spoken word had great power and strengthened the magic of the runes to bring success in spell-working. But the way in which the words were spoken was vital, poetry being the most potent because of the special skills required to master it, both memory and correct delivery.

Poetry was regarded as a magical force even when not accompanied by a runic inscription, and in Norse tradition a skilled poet was believed to be capable of bringing about physical effects through his verse, as in the tale of Thorleif and Jarl Hakon. The latter had burnt Thorleif's ship, so in the guise of a beggar he entered Jarl's hall to take revenge. There, Thorleif uttered a cursing poem that caused Jarl to lose his beard and the hair on one side of his head, and to develop an itch between his legs. The force of the poem also caused the sudden death of several men and plunged the hall into darkness.

Word Power and Runemasters

As the Teutonic tradition was an oral one, the majority of the population would not have been literate. This meant that the skills of rune cutters and runemasters were much in demand. And, due to the fact that the runes were unintelligible to most people, they were naturally regarded with a sense of awe, as were those who worked with them, to a greater or lesser extent.

People from all walks of life - for example farmers, craftsmen and merchants - could be rune cutters, as this simply demanded the ability to read and carve the characters. Whereas the runemasters were skilled magicians, exceptional members of society who carried great prestige. They understood the powers of the letters on all levels, and their application of them far exceeded the mere carving of inscriptions.

Both men and women could become runemasters. The Teutonic peoples credited women with great magical gifts, so that male sorcerers were usually trained by women. It is not known what form the training of a runemaster took, though it would have been oral from master/mistress to pupil, and might possibly have involved an initiation symbolically re-enacting Odin's self-sacrifice. Not only would the runemaster have to be skilled at understanding, reading and carving the runes on a material level, he or she would also have to master the poetic and occult arts and be adept at divination.

Runemasters could work magic with the runes to widely differing ends, from healing to cursing, as is shown in mythology and from inscriptions. Each rune was believed to have an associated spirit or energy, which had to be carefully controlled by the runemaster. Also, it was essential to fully understand the application of runic formulae before attempting to carry out any magical working, or the outcome could be unexpected or even dangerous.

The tales of the famous Skald and runemaster, Egil Skallagrimsson, demonstrate the wide scope of the runes when employed by a skilled initiate. On one occasion he was called to the bedside of a girl dangerously ill with fever, only to discover that a peasant boy, with good intentions but lacking the proper training, had already carved runes onto a piece of whalebone which had been placed in the patient's bed. When Egil saw that the inscription was harmful, he rapidly scratched it out and burnt the whalebone, replacing it with the correct formula which soon brought about the girl's recovery.

Egil also saved his own life through the use of runes. When given a horn of wine by Gunnhild, the witch wife of the Viking Erik Bloodaxe, later King of Northumbria, Egil suspected it was poisoned. He carved runes around the rim of the drinking horn, stained them with his own blood and recited a magical verse. When the horn burst, due to the power of the runes, his suspicions were confirmed.

At a later date, Egil was again in conflict with Gunnhild and Erik, and constructed a cursing pole by means of rune magic. He placed a horse's head on a hazel staff, then cursed Erik and Gunnhild, summoning spirits to drive them from the land. He finished by placing the pole in the ground and carving runes upon it. Another tale, written down by the Christian historian Bede, tells how a Northumbrian captive escaped by mysterious means. On being re-captured he was asked if he knew the formula for loosening bonds and if he had runes concealed about his person.

In the 'Runatál' Odin himself says that he can escape any bonds by means of runic incantation, using the power of sound vibration rather than cutting the letters. The 'Runatál' also contains seventeen other charms showing how runes can be employed for magical purposes, for example: to lift the spirits, for healing, for protection in battle, to counteract curses, in weather magic, to reanimate a corpse, and to win a lover. One verse of runic instruction in the same poem states, 'Better not to slay, than to slay too many', showing that the runes could be put to deadly purpose, but that the indiscriminate use of such power would in the end only bring harm to the runemaster.

Magical Runic Inscriptions

The archaeological evidence for runic inscriptions is found on both mobile and fixed objects, on which the letters were usually carved in order to obtain magical protection or power. Runes occur on such artefacts as brooches, spearheads, swords, protective amulets, drinking horns and statuettes, to name but a few.

Inscribing a spearhead or shaft was thought to aid the weapon's deadliness in battle. For example, the iron blade with silver inlay found at Dahmsdorf is inscribed on both sides, one depicting magical symbols, the other bearing Elder Futhark characters spelling 'Ranja' (the Runner), the name of the spear. As name and nature were magically linked, the intention was to enhance the spear's power to 'run the enemy through'.

156

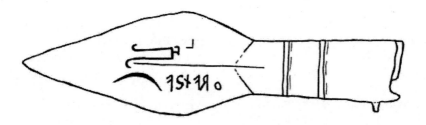

14. The Dahmsdorf spearhead, bearing a runic inscription which reads 'ajnar'. When read in reverse this spells 'ranja', the magical name of the spear.

When brooches were inscribed the function was less sinister, the runes being created in order to bring good luck or for magical protection.

Thirdly, runic inscriptions often occur on the thin gold disks called bracteates which were probably used for talismanic purposes. These had letters stamped onto the surface, often along with a design from a Roman coin depicting an Emperor, though, in the Teutonic tradition the figure was seen as Odin or Balder. In the Sievern Bracteate the parallel lines emanating from the figure's mouth are interpreted by the expert Karl Hauck as the magical breath and word-power of which Odin was master.

The Elder Futhark is also found on rock faces, carved with the purpse of sanctifying or protecting the place. The usual method was for the runemaster to assume the identity of a deity, then to carve the runes of his magical name whilst divinely inspired.

In addition, inscriptions were carved on the dressed stones known as 'bauta stones', associated with the cult of the dead over which Odin presided. The wording on the seventh century example from Björketorp in Sweden curses any desecrator with death, the runes having been magically imbued with the runemaster's will. Inscriptions were also intended as a protection against sorcerers, or to stop the dead from walking. Alternatively, runes could be employed to contact or summon the dead for magical purposes.

Certain stones of the same period had inscriptions carved on the inner side instead, where they were hidden from sight, for example the fourth century Kylver stone from Gotland, Sweden, which formed part of grave. The inscription may have been intended to prevent the ghost from troubling the living, or for the benefit of the soul in the next world. This is a possibility, as runes were sometimes placed beneath the tongue of the deceased to help him or her reply correctly to Odin's questions in the Afterworld Thing, or decision-making assembly.

Like the Elder Futhark, Anglo-Saxon runes are found on an assortment of objects, such as the scabbard mount from Chessel Down which bears an inscription translated as 'increase pain'. The interesting fact about this inscription is that it is concealed on the inner side of the mount, and therefore invisible. The efficacy would be increased by its secret nature, and a well-known occult principle might also have been applied here. After the rite had been performed and the talismanic inscription carved, it was then consciously forgotten in order for it to work its magic through the subtle realms.

In mythology, magical rings inscribed with runes are credited with great powers such as making the magician invisible, giving him the ability to fly or protecting him from harm. Such a ring, engraved with thirty runes, was discovered at Greymoor Hill in Cumbria, with three of the runes on the inner side and twenty seven on the outer.

Many memorial stones bear testament to Viking Age runic practice. Instead of being part of the grave, as with the earlier bauta stones, they are often found separately, and are commemorative in nature. The Swedish Strö Stone, dating to around 1000, is an example of such a memorial, dedicated to a man named Asser who met his death while on a viking expedition.

Sometimes single runes were inscribed for magical purposes, their names and meanings used symbolically to effect a result. For example Teiwaz, representing the name and powers of the war god Tyr, was often inscribed on weapons to gain his assistance in battle, while on the Skodberg bracteate the Jera rune is used as a talisman to obtain a good harvest. Elder Futhark runes are also sometimes found as ideographs in a Younger Futhork inscription, such as Dagaz occuring in a Younger inscription from Ingoldstat in Sweden, dated to the tenth century.

Carving the whole Futhark was another magical practice, evidence of which has been found on artefacts from all periods including the Middle Ages, giving us the correct letter order for the various runic systems. An example of the complete Elder Futhark is found on the Kylver Stone, dated to around 400 AD, while the Thames Scramaseax from around 700 AD shows the entire Anglo-Saxon Futhork. Confusingly, the letter sequence on the scramaseax does not follow the usual Anglo-Saxon order, as found in the 'Anglo-Saxon Rune Poem', which corresponds to the Elder Futhark sequence. Therefore, it is believed that the scramaseax Futhork was copied from elsewhere by the swordsmith, who was not versed in rune-lore.

Some experts suggest that these complete Futharks are teaching aids, but many probably had a magical purpose. As the full set of runes in their correct sequence stands for completeness - the symbols being representative of all things - and order, the carving of them could well have been carried out to bring about magical control and order on either the material or spiritual level.

Some inscriptions appear to be non-sensical, either they are unpronounceable or simply do not spell known words. However, they may represent, in effect the opposite of the full Futhark row. Whereas this encourages the establishment of order, the nonsensical inscriptions may represent the forces of chaos. Alternatively, they may be some form of magical language known only to the ancient runemasters.

Runic Conventions and Methods

In the 'Runatál' section of the Norse poem 'Hávamál', traditionally composed by Odin, instructions are given for the magical use of runes. These involve eight important steps: cutting, reading, staining, proving, asking, sacrificing, sending and destroying. The first two are self-explanatory, but the practice of staining is less well-known.

Runic inscriptions were usually coloured, the most popular colour being red. Pigments such as red oxide and ochre were used as a substitute for blood, though the actual substance of life was preferred, as shown in 'Egil's Saga', where the hero stains the runes around the rim of the poisoned drinking horn with his own blood as an essential step in the magical method of testing the contents. The blood had to be the runemaster's and none other, effecting a symbolic sacrifice and creating a magical connection with the working.

Runes could also be tinted blue, white, black and brown. The purpose of colouring was chiefly magical, though sometimes it was used to create a striking artistic effect or to divide words, with different sections of an inscription tinted different colours.

Once a magical inscription had been cut, its effectiveness, and the skill of the runemaster, could only be proved by the result of the working - each success adding to the runemaster's reputation.

Asking, or invoking the assistance of the gods, was the fifth important step. The sixth indicates that actual sacrificial rites may have been a part of rune magic, or perhaps the sacrifice was symbolic and had a close connection to staining with the runemaster's blood.

After the above steps had been carried out the spell was 'sent', released to do its work, a process which would have involved the use of the spoken word, intoning rune names, words of power or magical verse. Finally, once a rune formula had been sent, its physical form was destroyed in order for the power to be transferred. Alternatively, the runes might be destroyed in order to stop the spell from being activated, as in Egil's healing rite.

The 'Runatál' instructions also give warnings against the misuse of rune-magic, telling would-be runemasters not to demand too much or they will have to pay the price, as no magical success comes without personal sacrifice. Nor must they use the power of the runes for evil purposes:

'Better not to ask them to overpledge

as a gift demands a gift,

better not to slay,

than slay too many.'

Finally, the verse ends with the lord of inspiration telling the trainee runemaster that the skills and power she or he seeks will only be achieved with time and dedication.

Cryptic Systems

The runemasters were also skilled in the use of various cryptic systems, not only for the purpose of confusing potential readers, but in order to add to the power of the working. The more obscure the formula, the further from the realms of normal human understanding, the greater the effect in occult terms.

The letters of the Futhark and Futhork sequences were divided into groups known as 'ættir', a name which has several meanings including 'eight', and which derives from the Icelandic word 'ætt'. The Elder Futhark was divided into three such groups, each containing eight runes; the twenty eight letters of the Anglo-Saxon Futhork were split into four groups, three with eight letters and the fourth with only four; while the sixteen letter Viking Futhork was divided into aettir of six, five and five letters respectively, each group named after a god or goddess: Freya, Hagal and Tiw/Tyr.

Most cryptic methods were based on the ætt system discussed above. These operated by using the number of the ætt in which the relevant rune was found, and the number where that rune was placed in the ætt counted from the left. One set of strokes, sometimes in the form of a symbolic object, would represent the ætt, the other the rune position.

An example of such a system is:

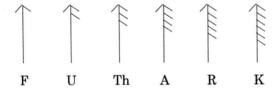

F   U   Th   A   R   K

Alternatively, a formula could be disguised by moving the letter values along one in the Futhark row so that the rune Uruz, usually representing U, would stand for F, Fehu in the Elder Futhark. Sometimes single runes were used as ideographs for their names, or letters, such as all the vowels, were omitted. Changing the letter order or substituting symbols for runes was also a way of achieving obscurity.

One form of symbol frequently employed was the bind-rune, an amalgamation of two separate runes, used either as a cryptic code or in magical workings to combine the forces of two runes in one sigil.

Runic Numerology

Number lore was important to the early Teutonic peoples and was therefore employed in rune magic, though runic numerology differs from Greek or Hebrew in that each letter does not possess a number value. Instead, the numerological significance lies in the groupings of the letters. Repetition was believed to give rise to powerful magic, but the meaning of the number formula depended on the interpretation of the runes involved and the general context of the inscription. The total number of letters carved was also relevant, for example five letters promised success. If the number of runes in the completed inscription was not appropriate to a working it could be shortened by combining two letters in a bind-rune, or lengthened by the addition of a symbol such as the swastika - an ancient solar symbol.

The most important numbers in runic numerology were three and eight. A rune had to be written three times for a lesser invocation of gods or demons. Additionally, three was the number of activation, and was used in connection with the troll rune, Thurisaz. This character was written three times in order to change the meanings of the three letters which followed it in a magical inscription.

Eight was also a number of activation, and of strength. As the largest number of repeated runes ever found in a sequence, it stood for ultimate fulfilment and completion. When a rune was repeated eight times this constituted a greater invocation.

Divination by Rune

The Norns

Associated with the runes in their divinatory role were the three sister goddesses known as the Norns, who governed the fate or 'wyrd' of humankind, weaving the web of destiny.

Like the Pagan Triple Goddess, the Norns were connected with the phases of the moon in Teutonic belief. Urd, who was visualized as an old woman, presided over the past, and was linked to the waxing moon; Verdanki, who ruled the present, was seen as a young maiden looking directly ahead and was related to the full moon; while Skuld, who was veiled and carried a scroll on which the future was written, was linked to the waning moon.

It was chiefly to Skuld that the runemasters would turn, though she was often regarded with dread, having the capacity to symbolically rip apart the web of destiny which her sisters had so carefully woven.

Rune Casting

The reports of classical writers, such as Ceasar and Tacitus, confirm that the runes were used for divinatory purposes. Tacitus, writing in 98 AD, describes the method, 'They cut a branch from a fruit tree and cut it into strips, marking them with distinctive signs. Then they scatter the pieces at random on a white cloth. An official priest (if it is a matter of tribal importance) or the head of the household (if it is a private matter) prays to the gods and, looking up into the sky, picks up three sticks one at a time and interprets them in accordance with the signs carved on them.'

Though in the past runes had many sacred functions, today they are chiefly associated with divination, and the modern method differs little from that of the early runemasters. Birch, ash and yew are traditionally the best woods for making the rune staves, which can be kept in draw-string pouch.

In order to cast the runes they can either be shaken in the pouch and the questioner asked to select a certain number, or else they can be physically cast onto a cloth as in Tacitus' report. Those that fall face up are then read. Alternatively, the whole set of runes can be laid out and 'shuffled' before a number are selected.

A reading of three runes chosen by one of the above means is a good method, three being the number used in ancient times according to both Ceasar, writing in 55 BC, and to Tacitus. Though there is no limit to the numbe of layouts which can be devised by the runecaster.

Interpretation of the Runes

The names of the runes come to us from the rune poems which were written down between the eighth and fifteenth centuries, though these date from a period many years after runes were first in use they derive from earlier oral sources. In the early days a rune name would have been important as the synthesis of all the correspondences associated with that rune, and it would also have helped recall the symbol and sound value.

Not only the rune names, but also the symbolic meanings of the runes are revealed in the rune poems. In these poems the verses follow the standard rune order, each verse explaining the rune with which it begins. The 'Anglo-Saxon (or Old English) Rune Poem' is important as it deals with the twenty-nine letter Anglo-Saxon Futhork and gives the meanings of the Elder Futhark runes, for which there is no surviving poem. The 'Old Norwegian Rune Rhyme' from the late twelfth century and the 'Old Icelandic Rune Poem' from the fifteenth century - though deriving from a far older tradtition - both deal with the interpretation of the sixteen letter Viking Futhork.

The following interpretations are based on the lore contained in these rune poems, using the names and symbols of the Elder Futhark. See table for the names belonging to the Anglo-Saxon and Viking traditions.

Rune	Letter	Name	Meaning		Rune	Letter	Name	Meaning
ᚠ	F	FEOH	Wealth		ᛋ	S	SIGEL	Sun
ᚢ	U	UR	Aurochs		ᛏ	T	TIR	Tyr
ᚦ	Th	ThORN	Thorn		ᛒ	B	BEORC	Birch
ᚩ	O	OS	God/Mouth		ᛖ	E	EH	Horse
ᚱ	R	RAD	Riding		ᛗ	M	MAN	Man
ᚳ	C	CEN	Torch		ᛚ	L	LAGU	Ocean
ᚷ	G	GYFU	Gift		ᛝ	Ng	ING	Ing
ᚹ	W	WENNE	Bliss		ᛞ	D	DAEG	Day
ᚻ	H	HAEGL	Hail		ᛟ	E	EThEL	Estate
ᚾ	N	NYD	Need		ᚪ	A	AC	Oak
ᛁ	I	IS	Ice		ᚫ	AE	AESC	Ash
ᛄ	J	GER	Year		ᚣ	Y	YR	Bow?
ᛇ	Y	EOH	Yew		ᛠ	IO	IAR	Otter?
ᛈ	P	PEORD	Chessman		ᛠ	EA	EAR	Grave?
ᛉ	Z	EOLH	Sedge					

The Anglo-Saxon Futhork

Fehu - Cattle
In early socitics cattle were associated with wealth, a man's or tribe's prosperity being largely determined by the head of cattle owned. Therefore, in divination this rune indicates material gain and worldly possessions. The 'Anglo-Saxon Rune Poem' also suggests that the wealthy should be generous, a quality held in high regard by the Teutonic peoples. The Norse rune poems both declare that money is a cause of strife, as in the well-known saying 'money is the root of all evil'.

Fehu is linked to the goddess Freya, whose sacred animal is the ox.

Uruz - Aurochs
The aurochs, now extinct, was a breed of wild cattle, fierce, massive and possessing great strength and speed. Because of the qualities attributable to the animal, Uruz denotes strength and power in humans. The rune also relates to courage and the defence of what a person values. Thirdly, it can stand for achievement, because in the past hunting and bringing down such a powerful animal was indeed a major feat.

Thurisaz - Troll or Thorn
The exact ancient meaning of this rune is uncertain, but it is usually seen as symbolizing unpleasant phenomena, amongst them giant, troll and thorn. In the 'Anglo-Saxon Rune Poem' the latter is described.

As mentioned above, Thurisaz is the troll rune, and when repeated three times it brings about reversal in the meaning of the runes following it. It is interpreted with the general meaning of difficulties, such as conflict, aggression, change and uncertainty.

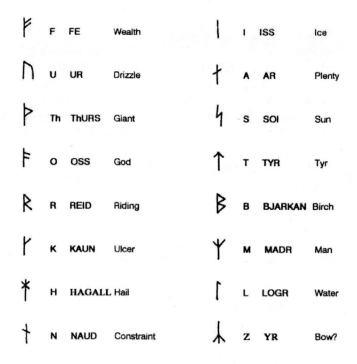

ᚠ	F	FE	Wealth		ᛁ	I	ISS	Ice
ᚢ	U	UR	Drizzle		ᛆ	A	AR	Plenty
ᚦ	Th	ThURS	Giant		ᛋ	S	SOI	Sun
ᚮ	O	OSS	God		ᛏ	T	TYR	Tyr
ᚱ	R	REID	Riding		ᛒ	B	BJARKAN	Birch
ᚴ	K	KAUN	Ulcer		ᛘ	M	MADR	Man
ᚼ	H	HAGALL	Hail		ᛚ	L	LOGR	Water
ᚾ	N	NAUD	Constraint		ᛦ	Z	YR	Bow?

The Viking Futhork

Ansuz - God or Mouth

In the 'Anglo-Saxon Rune Poem' this rune is written Os, and is described as the source of all language, bringing comfort, hope and happiness. In the poem there is also a verse for Aesc, the Anglo-Saxon name for the 'ae' rune. Aesc means the ash tree, the usual earthly symbol for the Norse World-Tree, Yggdrasil, on which Odin hung in order to obtain the runes.

Ansuz is associated with Odin, chief of the Aesir, god of the word and of wisdom, also linking this rune with the ash tree. It is a beneficial rune bringing happiness, especially that inspired by spiritual belief.

Raido - Riding

With its meaning of riding, this rune is associated with travel. It is also associated with Thor, the god of thunder, two concepts that are linked in Norse mythology as Thor supposedly caused thunder by travelling across the sky in his wheeled chariot.

When interpreting Raido it can mean either a physical journey or the life path.

Kaunaz - Torch

The above is the Anglo-Saxon meaning for this rune. The Old Norwegian and Icelandic rune poems give it less pleasant connotations, such as boil or ulcer. Either way, a burning torch or the fever accompanying disease produces the heat associated with Kaunaz. In divination it can be an indication that the querent has to be wary of ill health.

Gebo - Gift

Gebo is linked with gifts and generosity. It can be interpreted from the verse in the 'Anglo-Saxon Rune Poem', the only poem to feature this letter, as either the sacrifices made by humankind to the gods, or the gifts bestowed on humankind by them.

Therefore, Gebo is literally the giving of gifts or charity, or any exchange, including financial transactions.

Wunjo - Joy

This is a very favourable rune, indicating the lack of any troubles and the possession of happiness and material comfort. It denotes success and pleasure, but over-indulgence or extravagance must be guarded against.

Hagalaz - Hail

As Hagalaz is associated with savage weather which could destroy crops, it is seen as destructive. The weather is beyond the control of humans and is therefore linked with the forces of chaos. When interpreting Hagalaz these chaotic forces can be seen as within, disrupting the individual's equilibrium, or as outside factors which are not able to be controlled.

Nauthiz - Need

This rune relates to poverty, hardship and limitation, but conversely could also provide assistance. In ancient Teutonic belief it was thought to bring help if scratched on a fingernail. Nauthiz is also a rune of fate, linked to the Norns.

In a modern reading, as in the ancient poems, lack of money or comfort is indicated.

Isa - Ice

Hail is a violent natural force, whereas ice is static, binding and limiting. Therefore, Isa is a restrictive rune, indicating that the querent has to free him or her self from inner limitations.

Jera - Year or Harvest

In the rune poems Jera is associated with plenty and abundance, fulfulment after a good harvest. Similarly, it can be read in a modern context as the harvesting of what a person has planned and prepared for, the fruits of the querent's labours. Jera indicates prosperity and success.

Eihwaz - Yew
Yew was regarded as the best wood on which to carve runes and was also used to fashion bows for war or hunting. In Teutonic mythology the World Tree on which Odin sacrificed himself, though usually said to be an ash, is occasionally described as a yew.

Because the yew is associated with death, Eiwaz is sometimes referred to as the 'death rune'. However, the 'Old Norwegian Rune Rhyme' reminds us that the tree is an evergreen, in a sense deathless. This, together with the Odin myth, links Eihwaz to the concept of re-birth or transformation, as Odin sacrificed himself on the World Tree in order to receive the illumination of the runes.

The *'Anglo-Saxon Rune Poem'* refers to the yew as the keeper of the fire, which can be seen as the fire of the will, of perseverance, symbolized by the yew's survival of winter.

Pertho - Chessmen, Hearth, Dance, Fruit Tree.....?

The rune Pertho is very ambiguous, with a bewildering variety of meanings attributed to it. The interpretation of chessmen comes from the 'Anglo-Saxon Rune Poem', which associates it with recreation in the warriors' hall.

Some scholars link Pertho with the fertility goddess Frigg and female sexuality, and as such it can be interpreted as relating to women's mysteries and fertility. It can also relate to mysteries in general, anything which is unknown.

Algiz - Protection
Algiz symbolizes defence and protection, and is related to the Old English word 'ealgian' meaning 'to protect'. This rune is associated with the elk, which ably protects itself with massive horns, while in the 'Anglo-Saxon Rune Poem' the relevant verse describes a prickly sedge grass which defends itself by causing pain to anyone trying to pick it.

Algiz can be read as the desire for protection and security. Also the desire to defend possessions and position in life.

Sowulo - Sun
As the bringer of light and the sustainer of life, the sun was revered by all ancient cultures, and its associated rune was endowed with positive qualities. For the Teutonic peoples the sun was also represented by the swastika or sun wheel, depicting the yearly round of the seasons. In a reading Sowulo means good health, vigour and general happiness.

Teiwaz - Tyr
This rune is associated with the war god Tyr, who exemplified honour and who was a strong protector. For this reason Teiwaz was often engraved on amulets. It is also frequently found on cremation urns.

Teiwaz can be seen as the phallic symbol of male energy, used in a positive way. Just as Tyr brought victory in battle, this rune signifies success in disputes or in any of life's endeavours. It also denotes positive direction and leadership.

Berkana - Birch
For the early Teutonic peoples the birch was the tree of spring, associated with fertility and symbolic of growth. Berkana is a fortunate rune which denotes development on all levels, fertility and good news. Anything that is started will prosper when Berkana is cast.

Ehwaz - Horse

The horse was both valued in worldly life and held sacred by ancient peoples. Odin rode a supernatural eight-legged stallion named Sleipnir, and the horse was sacred to Frey, god of fertility.

The 'Anglo-Saxon Rune Poem' describes the pride men take in their horses, then says that a horse 'is always a comfort to the restless.' These lines give Ehwaz its divinatory meaning of status; and of change and movement, such as a new job or home.

Mannaz - Man

Mannaz is associated either with the self or with humankind. The 'Anglo-Saxon Rune Poem' describes the bond of kinship, and the 'Old Icelandic Rune Poem' focuses on the positive nature of man, however, both remind the reader of human mortality.

In a casting Mannaz can be interpreted as the querent's relationship with others, both positive and negative, and mutual influence.

Laguz - Water

According to the various rune poems Laguz is associated with either the wide ocean, with a waterfall or a lake. It is sacred to the Vanir god, Njord.

In a reading Laguz can denote travel, or the realm of imagination, dreams and psychic matters, which are associated with the watery element. As the 'Norwegian Rune Rhyme' mentions gold, Laguz can also relate to material gain.

Inguz - Fertility

Inguz is the rune of the fertility god Frey, but when cast in a reading it relates to the family and children as well as to male fertility.

Dagaz - Day or Dawn
The day is associated with light and optimism, therefore, Dagaz has positive connotations. It signifies opportunity and improvement in life's circumstances, the dawn of new beginnings.

Othila - Estate
This rune relates to the ancestral home and ancestral lore, with the 'Anglo-Saxon Rune Poem' describing the importance of a man's estate.

In a reading the meanings are similar: home, inheritance, ancestry and heritage.

Modern Runic Uses

Besides being employed for divination, runes can also be used in the creation of talismans, or for meditation and pathworking.

The writing of the characters as part of a ritual working requires concentration and application, adding to the potency of the words, whether written on paper or carved on a candle. Runes can be also be inscribed on protective amulets or on talismans, in the latter case the use of a bind-rune is especially appropriate to concentrate the power as much as possible.

The symbolic meanings of the runes provide illuminating meditation subjects, as do runic inscriptions and verses from the rune poems or literature such as 'Runatál'. Visualizing the rune and its interpretation develops insight on all levels, so that a deeper understanding can be reached. Alternatively, runes can be used in pathworking - see Chapter Two for guidelines - in which a sequence of events can be based around the symbolism of a chosen rune or bind-rune.

As with other sacred alphabets, the runes are not a system relevant only to the past, and the more they are worked with, either for divination or in meditation, the more their many levels of meaning will become apparent.

Chapter Seven

In the Realm of Magic

Esoteric Alphabets

The earliest alphabets, whether sacred or mundane, always belonged to distinct areas or tribes. Then, during the Middle Ages, when the alphabets in current use had mostly lost their sacred associations, a new form of alphabet came into being, the magical script.

Occultists of this period and later employed magical alphabets for much the same reasons as the Egyptian scribes, Teutonic runemasters and bardic writers of Ogham did before them. In an age when literacy was more widespread, at least amongst the wealthier classes, a script was needed which set magical workings apart from the secular uses of writing, the study and concentration giving added potency to the work, the unfamiliar opening a door that could change perception. Also, the desire for secrecy obviously played a part. By employing magical scripts occultists could communicate with other initiates without divulging potentially dangerous knowledge.

A feature of Medieval magic is the grimoire, a volume containing lengthy instructions for magical preparation and the conjuration of spirits, and it is in these that the magical alphabets are usually found. There are dozens in existence, invented or 'received' by Medieval and post-Medieval occultists, the letters sometimes based on alchemical and astrological symbolism, as well as on existing alphabets such as the Hebrew or Greek.

Of these alphabets the Enochian, otherwise known as the Malachim, is one of the most important, and it is not only an

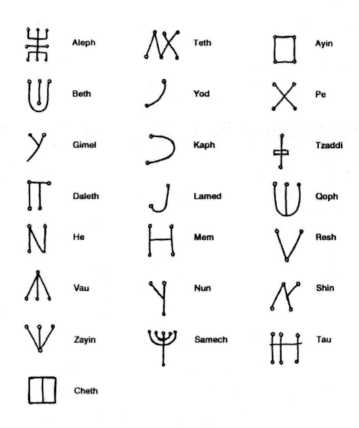

	Aleph		Teth		Ayin
	Beth		Yod		Pe
	Gimel		Kaph		Tzaddi
	Daleth		Lamed		Qoph
	He		Mem		Resh
	Vau		Nun		Shin
	Zayin		Samech		Tau
	Cheth				

The Enochian or Malachim Script

alphabet but a language, made famous by Dr John Dee (1527-1608) and his seer, Edward Kelley. Dee, scholar, occultist, and court astrologer to Queen Elizabeth I, had ambitions of discovering the alchemical Philosopher's Stone or of finding buried treasure by means of spirit communication, however, as he himself lacked sufficient psychic powers, he needed someone to 'scry' for him. For this he chose the roguish Kelley, a man who had once been in serious trouble with the law. But, whatever his past, the Irishman was a natural psychic, who was able to see visions and hear spirit voices after gazing into a 'shew stone' or crystal ball.

According to Dee, the faint outlines of the Enochian letters appeared on parchment during one of Kelley's trances, and were later inked over by Dee for greater clarity. But, in truth, his inspiration came from Pantheus' *Voarchadumia*, an old volume in Dee's possession, containing a sacred script which he adopted for his own Enochian system of angelic communication.

Through his spirit contacts Kelley received a series of charts divided into squares, with a letter of the alphabet in each square. Copies of these charts were made, and when he went into trance Kelley would see an angel pointing to a sequence of squares. He would relate his vision to Dee who recorded the messages using his own copy of the chart. According to the spirits, the Enochian words and messages possessed immense power, and they were often given backwards to prevent forces from being unleashed which might disrupt the communication.

Occultists, including Aleister Crowley, who worked with the conjurations or 'Keys' received, have confirmed the potency of Enochian and note that it is a true language with grammar and syntax, not simply a jumble of words. The words consist mainly of consonants, as in the Hebrew alphabet, with the vowel sounds vocalized according to the rules of the language.

Another sacred alphabet of special interest is the Theban Alphabet of Honorius, named after the legendary magician, which is still in use today, especially amongst witches. The

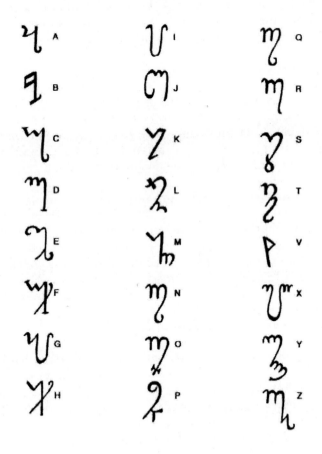

The Theban Alphabet

reason for this is probably because the Theban script is based on Latin characters rather than the more usual Hebrew, and therefore fits in with a practice that does not as a rule employ Qabalistic methods.

The Apollonian Script, claimed to have been invented by the ancient magician Apollonius of Tyana, is largely based on Greek characters, while several major esoteric scripts are inspired by the Hebrew alphabet. These include the Celestial - or Heavenly - Script (Scriptura Coelestis), Passing the River (Transitus Fluvii) and the Writing of the Magi. The latter three alphabets were collected by the Qabalist and mystic, Cornelius Agrippa (1486-1535).

Medieval occult alphabets were put to practical magical use in the conjuration of spirits to do the magician's will. They feature on talismans, and were inscribed around magical circles drawn for protection and as a demarcation of sacred space.

Like the scripts themselves, Medieval ceremonial magic was largely based on the Qabalistic tradition, though various Pagan beliefs, espcially those of the classical civilizations, also played a part. Complex rules surrounded the performance of such rites, which required careful preparation. The correct position of the planets in relation to the work was essential, as were number and colour correspondences. Written symbols or conjurations gained power and potency by being in occult lettering, and the materials used were also specified. *The Grimoire of Honorius* prescribes virgin parchment, meticulously prepared, while the famous medieval grimoire known as *The Key of Solomon* gives instructions for writing on the skin of a hare with the blood of a black hen.

Like the magicians and priests who preceded them by thousands of years in ancient Egypt, Medieval ceremonial magicians used words of power in order to obtain their ends. Names of power, mainly those of the Hebrew god, were employed for protection and to command and subdue the spirits evoked. The importance of names is emphasized in the grimoires, not only those of the

The Writing of the Magi

biblical god, but of the spirits, who could only be commanded if their correct names were known, giving the magician complete power over them.

In the seventeenth and eighteenth centuries secret alphabets , such as the Sovereign Princes' Rose Cross Cipher, started to be used by Masonic and Rosecrucian orders. These Rosecrucian alphabets are based on a grid system, with each character shape depicting where the relevant Latin letter is placed on the grid. This system can give rise to many variations according to the form of grid used, making decipherment virtually impossible without access to the grid.

For example, the following grid relates to the alphabet in figure number 17:

A B C	D E F	G H I
J K L	M N O	P Q R
S T U	V W X	Y Z

Magical Squares

The use of letters or numbers inscribed within magical squares was another major component of Medieval and more recent ceremonial magic. An earlier example, the SATOR square, which originated in the Pagan period and carried over into Christianity, is shown in chapter five on the Roman tradition.

Magical squares, in conjunction with ritual, were used to bring about desired changes. Usually these squares were numerical, containing numbers relating to the planets and the spirits ruling them, however, in *The Book of the Sacred Magic of Abramelin the Mage* alphabetic squares play a major part.

This book is translated by S L MacGregor-Mathers, one time head of the Order of the Golden Dawn, from an eighteenth

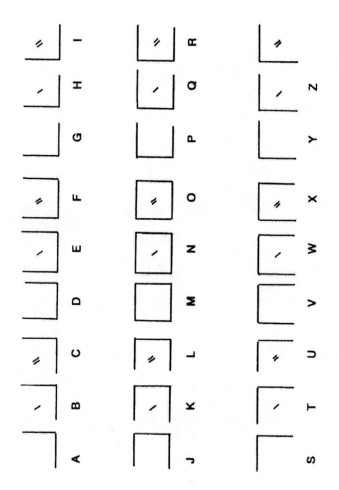

A Rose Cross Cipher

M	I	L	O	N
I	R	A	G	O
L	A	M	A	L
O	G	A	R	I
N	O	L	I	M

S	E	Q	O	R
E	Q	A	M	O
Q		S		Q
O			Q	
R		Q		

'Milon' and 'Sator' Magical Squares

century French translation of a Medieval manuscript, which he came across in the Biblioteque de l'Arsenal in Paris. The purported original was a grimoire of instructions written by Abraham the Jew for his son Lamech in 1458. Whether the French 'translator' really worked from a Medieval manuscript or not, whoever composed the text possessed a sound knowledge of Qabalistic ritual magic as practised in the Middle Ages.

The first two parts of the book consist of the preparation of the magician and place of working, while the final part contains well over two hundred magical squares. 'To know all manner of things Past and Future', Abraham tells the magician to 'take the Symbol in your hand, place it (upon the top of your head) under your hat, and either you will be secretly warned by the Spirit, or he will execute that which you have the intention of commanding him to do.'

The first square in figure number 18 relates to the above, and is an example of a double acrostic in which the words can be read from all directions. According to Mathers, the words contained in the square derive from different languages but basically describe the desired purpose, the point being to create a talisman in which the essence of the working is condensed and emphasized.

'To have as much gold and silver as one may wish', the symbol must be placed in the magician's purse, and after a short time the required money will materialize! The second square in figure number 18 is for obtaining gold coins, while another must be used if silver is wanted.

Most people these days do not expect the results of their working to be quite so direct. Usually, if someone creates a talisman for financial gain, he or she also opens up physical opportunities for the money to manifest, such as buying a lottery ticket or looking for promotion. Talismans used today take many forms, for many purposes. If you would like to pursue this further, several of the books listed in the bibliography give details for constructing a talisman, and also for the use of letters in various forms of occult work.

Chapter Eight

Influences

The influences of the word are many and varied, so rather than focusing on a specific tradition, in this chapter it is encountered from widely diverse angles. These range from the power of the sound vibration underlying speech and the subtle psychological effect of words used in everyday life, to spirit communication by means of automatic writing and character analysis through the physical shape of written letters.

The first influence is the basis of many creation myths, and its tremendous potential is backed up by scientific fact.........

The Power of Vibration

More than any other factor, it is the power of vibration that underlies the study of the spoken word, including chants and mantras - a power that can be harnessed for good, or which can prove highly dangerous if tampered with or abused.

Everything in the universe, animate and inanimate, is affected by vibration, and in the 1920s a Russian engineer named George Lakhovsky came up with the theory that vibration is the basis of all life, stating that 'cells, the essential organic units of all living bodies, emit and absorb high frequency waves.'

Sound, too, consists of vibrations which travel in waves, at varying speeds according to the type of sound. This is a highly technical subject, but to put it in a nutshell, infrasonics are extremely low frequency sound levels (vibrating and travelling slowly), while ultrasonics or supersonics are of a very high frequency. Between these two lies the range audible to the human ear, though some people's hearing is more acute that other's, while dogs can hear sounds with a higher frequency than most humans can.

To assist his researches, in the 1960s a French engineer named Professor Gavreau created a giant whistle capable of producing infrasonic sound, though he failed to realize the full extent of its devastating power until it was too late. On its initial testing the machine made his entire team ill and brought about the death of the operating technician, whose internal organs disintegrated as a result of the vibrations generated.

Earlier, in 1896, a mechanical oscillator invented by the engineer Nikola Tesla caused buildings in New York to shake as if in an earthquake. Gavreau, too, invented a machine which produced a similarly destructive effect, both cases reminiscent of Joshua and the walls of Jericho.

Through the use of vibration, scientists have also caused wood to catch fire, which brings to mind the threatening words of a fifteenth century Irish Chief Bard to the man who had burnt his corn, 'Even though the scorching of your handsome face might well have been the outcome of the deed, it is not right to redden people's faces for the grain glowing dreadful in the fields.....' And there is an Indian tale which relates how the court musician of Akbar the Great, an emperor of the conquering Moghuls, caused a river to boil and the air to catch fire through his singing. Are these tales simply fantasy, or based on ancient knowledge?

Though all the more recent experiments into vibration and sonics involve technical instruments, it is possible that the human voice could act in a similar way, with the appropriate natural gift, physical power and intense training. The production of vibration relies on the resonator, for example the pipes in a church organ. In a human being the resonators are the mouth, the nasal and head cavities and the breast bone.

Everything possess its own keynote, as was demonstrated by the operatic tenor Enrico Caruso. After flicking a wine glass to create a note, he then reproduced it with his voice, causing the glass to shatter. A variation on this theme are the studies of Dr Oscar Brunler earlier this century, who found that he could cure patients with vibration but that it had to be specific, ie. the vibrational frequency of the patient's own voice.

Mantras

The Indian yogis have known about the immense power of sound vibration for thousands of years, a knowledge put into practice through the use of mantras. These can consist of a sound, a syllable, a word or a significant phrase repreated constantly, either aloud or silently. Yogis skilled in the art have been credited with performing cures over vast distances through mantra-yoga, from ancient times through to the present, men such as the twentieth century 'poison king' Duraiswami Iyer who could cure a snakebite victim hundreds of miles away.

Since the 1960s many people in the west have become aware of the power of mantras, especially through their popular use in Transcendential Meditation for healing and relaxation, which is effective even without the meditator being trained in yogic discipline.

Besides being used to cure all manner of disease, mantras are also created to improve psychic powers or, most importantly, to increase spiritual awareness. It is essential that the mantra is intoned properly to achieve a balanced effect. The mantra AUM, often written OM, is the most universally powerful, and is sacred to the Hindus as the embodiment of their religious philosophy. The three letter sounds in order correspond to the Hindu trinity of gods: Brahma the Creator, Vishnu the Preserver and Shiva the Destroyer. Therefore, this manta embodies the three as one and the one as three. The three letters also represent body, soul and spirit, in addition to many other triple concepts. For the Hindus, as for the Druids, the number three enshrines a wealth of esoteric philolsophy.

When intoned, the final 'm' sound of AUM is produced as a hum, trailing off to inaudibility. This prolonged sound relates to pure consciousness, which the mystic aims to achieve. In a similar way the Christian 'Amen' and the Druidic 'Awen' also produce vibrations when intoned, leading towards spiritual enlightenment.

Speech, chanting and singing vary in frequency and therefore produce different effects on all levels, not only the physical, as thoughts also consist of vibration.

When a large crowd of people chant together it is well known that the effect is so powerful that it can lead to riot and violence. Though, of course, group chanting is also a part of much religious worship, creating a united sense of spiritual elevation rather than a negative result.

Many normally rational people report feeling out of control, unable to act calmly or to use their sense of reason when in the midst of a hysterical crowd, even if they do not feel particularly strongly about whatever the group is concentrating on. A typical example is the crowd violence which has increasingly come to marr football matches.

The qabalist and occultist Dion Fortune puts this effect down to the 'group mind', automatically created when a number of people focus on one idea which the majority are fanatical about. This group mind is in effect a form of entity built up by a number of highly focused individual minds, growing until it takes on a personality of its own, in turn influencing those that have created it to a greater intensity of feeling, 'sounding the note of its own being in their ears and thereby reinforcing the emotional vibration which originally gave it birth'. This explains how less interested participants can be drawn in as if hypnotized by the vibrations surrounding them. At each stage the increased passion of the crowd has the effect of adding to the power of the group mind, which continues to gain strength and in turn feeds the crowd.

Creating and directing this group mind so that it will influence vast numbers of people is where a skilled leader exercises his or her power. The crowd needs a focus, and here the chanting of a word or slogan combines the power of sound vibration and concentrated thought in much the same way as a mantra. The Nazis, who studied the occult arts to further their evil aims, were masters at this kind of mass manipulation, using such chants as 'Hail Hitler'.

But once the crowd disperses, and the individuals comprising it are no longer focused on a single idea, the group mind ceases to exist, so in order to create a more permanent group mind it is necessary to find a way of maintaining a certain level of attention and emotion. In this context slogans and symbols have a profound effect: national anthems, flags, or, again using the example of the Nazis, the swastika and the rune 'sowulo' for the SS. The power of ancient letters and archetypal symbols were imbued with a new significance by people who knew exactly how to apply psychology and the occult, using both sound and symbol in their techniques for brain-washing the populace.

Language

The choice and context of words read or heard also has the power to influence us, working at a subconscious level each time we encounter them. The way children are taught their language affects the way they regard the world, influencing them in later life.

Challenging our attitudes through the language we use, rather than just accepting antiquated conventions, can be constructive and progressive. It is only when valid ideas are taken to extremes in some instances of so-called 'political correctness' that they are laughed at and dismissed along with those that justly deserve ridicule.

This is a vast subject but I will use just one example of how language can affect our outlook, because this example is so universal and one that I have become very aware of in writing this book. Many people, including authors, still persist in using the pronoun 'he' when referring to people in general. This often crops up in books on anthropology, history and archaeology because any member of the species homo sapiens sapiens is known as 'man', whether male or female. So we get such statements as 'when man discovered the use of fire it aided his progress towards civilization', a literary trend that continues when describing human advancements into the present century. 'Mankind' or 'humans' is a more balanced way of expressing the same idea, or are we to believe that women are still living in the Stone Age?

The same terminology is also found in many general books: 'if your vetinarian cannot come to you, take the dog to him', and in a career book 'the professional accountant is a specialist.......He may work in public practice.....' etc, etc. I need not list any more examples, of which there are plenty.

Because the language we speak stems from a patriarchal tradition, where until recently women were not given a decent education and were prohibited from following careers or even from voting, naturally it places men at the forefront. Less than a century ago the vet or the accountant would have been a man but I feel that by continuing to use this kind of language we perpetuate the idea that men are intrinsically more powerful and successful.

Most people read 'he' and do not even think about it. Women do not usually feel excluded because they have grown up with this convention of language. But we do notice when the author of a more progressive book alternates between he and she when referring to members of a profession, for example. It lifts us out of our complacency. Changing all words with man in is not practical and verging on the obsessive, but I see no reason for any writer to refer to all people as 'he' simply for the sake of convenience. As languages and their usage changes over time I am sure this will too, but it does illustrate how general thought-patterns are bound up with the terms we use in everyday communication.

190

Consciously and subconsciously the word shapes us, as humans once shaped their thoughts into sounds and form.

The Written Word

The act of writing is always in a sense magical, providing a channel for the mind to make thoughts tangible and accessible to others. Taken further, it is also believed to serve as a channel for discarnate spirits, or for the true character of the person writing to come through.

Automatic Writing

In the practice of automatic writing messages are written down by the 'receiver' without his or her conscious involvement, the receiver merely acting as a tool for the communicating spirit, much as a pen aor word-processor is for a writer.

This type of spirit contact is often carried out by a medium in trance, performed 'under control', ie. of the spirit. At other times the receiver is conscious yet does not consciously affect what is being written, instead endeavouring to keep his or her mind blank so as not to influence the communication.

Many works in the occult field are said to have been received through this method, but an example relating to the practical science of archaeology is especially interesting. In 1908 Frederick Bligh Bond, a well respected architect, was appointed trustee of the Glastonbury Abbey ruins after they had been purchased by the Church of England. He was also interested in psychic research, and acquainted with those who could perform automatic writing.

During one session an entity who claimed to be the spirit of a monk named Johannes Bryant (1497-1533) began to communiate through Bligh Bond's psychic friend. Writing in Saxon English and dog-Latin, the Medieval monk described the Abbey where he had been based and revealed details of side chapels not recorded in existing documents, giving precise measurements. Intrigued by these communications, Bligh Bond ordered excavations to be carried out in the areas indicated, and the foundations of several chapels were duly discovered, exactly as described by 'Johannes'.

Not surprisingly, the practice of communicating with disembodied spirits did not meet with the Church's approval, and in 1922 Bligh Bond was dismissed from his post, overshadowed by scandal.

Graphology

Graphologists believe that through the physical form of a person's handwriting the writer's own inner self, rather than an outside entity, is being 'channelled', enabling them to give a detailed character analysis from studying the letter shapes. They see the personality transmitted through the hand that writes, to be recorded on paper on a visible level, unconnected with the subject that is being written about. A person's signature is particularly relevant, unique like a fingerprint, and constantly changing as the character evolves throughout a lifetime.

Every aspect of the handwriting is examined: size, angle, pressure, spacing, loops, crossing of ts, and any unusual features.

Graphology can be regarded on a purely scientific basis, and is used for mundane purposes such as selecting the most appropriate candidates to call for interview from their writing on job application forms. But it is also reminiscent of ancient beliefs, where the essence of a person was transmitted through writing or inscribing. The northern runemasters invoked a magical personality upon themselves before doing their work in the belief that the magical potency would be transferred to the lettering.

When we write, our energy and emotions are not only directed into the subject matter but into the physical act of writing, in a sense we are pouring them, like the ink, through the pen.

Chapter Nine

Sacred Inspiration

Inspiration: to receive divine influence, to be blessed with a creative idea, to draw in breath. As the creator exhaled, vocalizing the divine name, so the universe came into being - the essence of belief in many traditions - and in this breath was, and is, the spirit of inspiration. So the Bard, the artist, the musician, metaphorically breathes this spirit in, taking it into him or herself. It is the Druidic 'Awen', and the Norse Poets' Share from the mead of inspiration dropped by Odin, the root of whose name means either 'wind' or 'spirit'. Direct awareness of divinity is linked with the gift of creativity, a sacred gift though of course not all creativity is inspired. Real inspiration is almost an intoxication, a moment when ideas arise with such force and clarity that they surprise the receiver, as if they have literally been drawn in from a higher source.

Ancient Greek epics, Celtic hero tales, Norse sagas and Medieval romances were fuelled by this fire of inspiration, which in turn fired the imagination of the audience. However, the early mythological tales were not regarded as fiction by those who heard them. Though the stories were fantastic, the adventures often happened to real people, or at least to people who were believed to have been real, who had lived in the remote past, to revered ancestors and deified heroes, not to invented characters. And, at a time when the supernatural was a part of everyday life nothing could be dismissed as pure invention. The audience were also literally a part of the tale. To the Celts, what was happening 'then' in the mythic past, was still happening 'now' in the eternal cycle of being. Time did not travel in a straight line, but events were played out in a cyclical way, where anyone could leap onto the wheel and join the gods and heroes, giving a sense of meaning, of belonging, the chance to encounter people and episodes that would now be described as archetypal.

The first chants, the first 'poetry' would have had a magico-religious function and would have been the province of the tribal shaman. The first mythological stories, too, were probably told by the shaman, in an attempt to make some sense of an existence that was both mysterious and dangerous, fraught with fear and death.

And who can say when human beings first sat around the fire, recounting the history of the tribe, the romance and the heroism? The tales themselves would soon have been seen to possess magical power, bringing the past to mind so clearly that it was relived time and again.

In the days when most people were illiterate, or in cultures such as the early Celtic where everything had to be committed to memory, verse acted as a mnemonic aid, and this format also helped to involve the audience with such devises as repeated refrains. The rhythm of poetry originally arose because it was once in effect a song lyric. Also, the rhythm and repetition acted on the audience like the hypnotic beat of the shaman's drum, guarding against distraction and opening people's minds to the marvels that were revealed, bringing about a change of consciousness.

Prose also had its birth at an early date. Around 2000 BC the ancient Egyptians told stories for pleasure, and tales dating from the fifth century BC were written in Greece, Babylonia and Persia. While later, from northern Europe, come the narrative prose compositions of the Irish and Norse sagas. Though the Medieval French courtly romances were composed in verse for a long period, they are examples of early popular fiction, and in the thirteenth century start to be found in prose as well.

The novel had its roots in the many sources mentioned above, developing through the novella - in length somewhere betwen a short story and a full-length novel - to a longer work of fiction. Cervantes (1547-1616), the Spanish writer of the famous *Don Quixote*, was a pioneer in the birth of the novel, which finally came of age in the eighteenth century.

These days, tales are not as a rule recited to a gathering of listeners by a trained storyteller, but read from the printed page, usually silently and alone. Yet the power of fiction has survived the centuries and the massive changes it has undergone because at the heart of storytelling nothing has in fact changed. It is a magical act.

In occult theory there are seen to be five levels of being: the spiritual, the mental, the astral, the etheric and the physical. The higher of these are sometimes subdivided into upper and lower spiritual, upper and lower mental, and upper and lower astral. In brief, the upper spiritual relates to the divine spark of life within all living beings, while the lower spiritual relates to the personal individual spirit or soul; the upper mental relates to the abstract mind, the lower mental to the concrete mind, the realm of logic; the upper astral is the plane of abstract emotions, the lower astral of instinct; while the etheric consists of non-dense matter, interwoven with the physical plane, holding it together and linking it with all the higher levels.

All magical ritual, other than pure worship, follows a basic pattern of: desire, form, manifestation. The desire is connected with the need to carry out a ritual, the purpose. It relates to the mental level of the magician in that it springs from an idea in the mind. Then, in order to develop it further it has to be defined, and the rite that will be performed must be carefully planned, still on the mental level which works with logic.

During the rite the desired result is clearly visualized, a process which corresponds to the astral level, the realm of dreams and visions, the door to the subconscious. The astral is the plane of imagination, its 'language' that of symbol and image rather than of words. It is where the blueprint for everything in the material world exists. Therefore, in a rite the astral counterpart of whatever the magician intends to influence is worked upon. Because, by its very nature, the astral is insubstantial and forever changing, it is also known as the plane of illusion.

The magician visualizes what he or she desires in minute detail before empowering these images by the force of emotion (also relating to the astral realm), and willpower. In a rite, words will be spoken aloud, vocalizing the desire and therefore employing sound vibration, though thoughts also possess a vibrational quality. This sequence then leads to the final stage of manifestation, when the desired objective materializes in the physical world of the five senses - though it does not literally have to be a physical object such as a new car but can be world peace, healing or an increase of knowledge.

The magician is in effect following the primal pattern of the divine creator as recalled in creation myths worldwide. The deity had a thought, a desire, a need. This thought was visualized, and vocalized in the creative word - the two happening more or less simultaneously as in a magical rite - and so the material world was born. This pattern can also be related to the realm of human artistic creativity.

In the course of writing fiction I have found that it produces results in the same way as performing a ritual. To give a few examples, I have created a fictional social circle and a precise scene, which a month later I found myself in, 'invented' a character who then walked into my life, and found an artefact around which the whole of my previous novel centred shortly after the novel had been completed.

At first this all came as both a surprise and a shock because I was not consciously aware of what I was doing, nor had I related the above method for performing a magical rite to the process of writing. But once you compare the two, the similarities are more than obvious.

Firstly, there is the basic idea for a novel or story which, through careful planning - in some cases at least! - is developed into a plot with three-dimensional characters and a location setting, real or imaginary. So far largely on the mental level, though naturally imagination also comes into the planning. But it is at the next stage that the mystery really begins.

As the author writes, he or she sees the characters and scenes as if on an inner cinema screen, and the black print on white paper becomes almost incidental. The author is seeing, feeling, recording and reporting on what is happening on an astral level. The more clearly the characters, places and events are visualized, the more power the work will have. After all, thoughts and images are all forms of vibration.

However one thing has been missing from these comparisons between magic and writing: inspiration, that illusive spark which apparently appears from an unknown source. True inspiration is not a product of the mental level. When it is experienced, it is a gift from the spiritual level, from the divine.

People from many traditions have believed in the power of the name, seeing it as an integral part of a person, so that knowledge of the true name was needed by anyone wishing to have power over an individual. In a similar way the names of characters in a novel encapsulate their essence, like a vessel into which everything that they are is poured.

And what is it exactly that is poured into these vessels? Possibly an already existent energy, seeking materialization. Mary Shelley, in her introduction to 'Frankenstein' says, 'Invention......does not consist in creating out of void, but out of chaos; the materials must, in the first place, be afforded: it can give form to dark, shapeless substances but cannot bring into being the substance itself.'

Certainly there is a great deal of the author's own self which also fills each vessel, both consciously and unconsciously. In the latter case the effect can be cathartic; 'demons' from the depths of the unconscious can emerge, while inner conflicts can be approached, played out and conquered like the Medieval knight slaying the dragon. And characters can display the writer's true strengths and gifts that circumstances have prevented from being shown in 'real' life, bringing them out into the light of day from safe but dusty corners.

The writer is not the only one affected on many levels by works of fiction. To hear or read a myth, a story or novel is to live temporarily in another world. As in the writing, the logical realm of words is transmuted to the imaginary and visionary world of images. The 'film' is re-run, though the effect is far richer and more personal than with a cinema film because each reader's inner film is different, coloured by his or her own imagination and needs.

The Celtic Bard or Norse Skald evoked the images for each member of a vast audience gathered in the chief's hall. The tales united the people, improving the tribe's morale giving a sense of common purpose but also of private realization. Through the events that were played out time and again, the listeners cont-acted their own subconscious and worked with the archetypes.

Writing is not only related to the performance of a magical rite, but is very similar to carrying out a pathworking. This also applies to reading or listening to a tale, except that the writer (apart from in the first person) or reader is watching the action rather than performing it. Besides providing the opportunity for identification and inspiration, fiction is also a form of meditation through escapism, by which we are carried into another world, onto the astral level where material concerns can be forgotton for the time being and returned to later with a fresh outlook. Being totally absorbed in a tale in effect brings about a change of conscious-ness.

But it is poetry, rather than fiction, which is generally credited with the power to change consciousness. It often contains hypnotic rhythm and rhyme and its symbolic and emotional content is more obvious, working largely with imagery. It is similar to the way in which a talisman works, condensing what is said to intensify its power.

In poetry, abstract and subtle glimmerings are shared. Also, love, pain, loss and happiness, to name but a few of the experiences we all go through at some time, can be expressed much more evocatively than in prose. People through the ages have been able to identify with these themes and apply them to their own lives, making the poem their own, as if they themselves had composed it.

A talented poet can express what we have all felt, but most of us cannot quite understand, let alone put into words. Through poetry we are able to look at ourselves, to get in touch with our feelings, not only those that bring pleasure but also those which are painful. Simply reading poetry is a form of meditation, and a poem, or even one line, can provide a rich source for longer, deeper meditation. The magic of poetry works directly on the subconscious and on the emotions, by-passing logical understanding, which makes it especially powerful.

Poetry and fiction, like mythology, give a purpose to existence, a feeling that each of us is not alone. Life only becomes meaningless when the poetic aspect, the symbolic world, is missing. We can choose to dismiss our lives as dull or stressful...... but there is another way of looking at the events, major or minor, that cross our paths.

Each life, even the most apparently mundane, is a story. If we see things in a mythological light we will see the true patterns behind them, and all things do possess a mythic quality. A hero or heroine is not always heroic, he or she often starts off as naive and foolish, it is the experiences, and notably the difficulties, faced that ultimately develop his or her potential. Identifying with a mythological hero/ine or a character in a current novel is a way to see the many layers of meaning in our own lives.

To experiment with this, try literally telling your own story, episodes in your life, to yourself as if you were a character in a myth or novel. What you might perceive as a failure is really a lesson on the route to empowerment, an adventure in fact. Or you could place yourself in the part of an existing mythological or fictional hero/ine, confronting the episodes they face, but in your own way. You take on the role of the Creator, the magician, the writer..............

Myth and so-called reality are entwined like a Celtic knot. Through the power of the imagination and of the sacred, creative word we can change not only ourselves but affect the world around us.

Bíblíogɾʌphy

Adkins, Lesley and Roy - *The Handbook of British Archaeology*, Macmillan, London, 1991.

Aldred, Cyril - *The Egyptians*, Thames & Hudson, London, 1984.

Baring, Anne and Cashford, Jules - *The Myth of the Goddess*, Penguin Arkana, London, 1993.

Baugh, Albert C and Cable, Thomas - *A History of the English Language'* (3rd edn.), Routledge & Kegan Paul, London, 1980.

Blake, N F - *'A History of the English Language'*, Macmillan, London, 1996.

Budge, Sir E A Wallis - *'Egyptian Language'*, Routledge, London, 1989 edn.

Budge, Sir E A Wallis - *'Egyptian Magic'*, Penguin Arkana, London, 1988 edn.

Ceram, C W - *'Gods, Graves and Scholars'*, Victor Gollancz, London, 1952.

Cheiro - *'Cheiro's Book of Numbers'*, Herbert Jenkins, London.

Crowley, Aleister - *'777 and Other Qabalistic Writings'*, Samuel Weiser, Maine, USA, 1986 edn.

Crowley, Aleister - *'The Book of Thoth'*, Samuel Weiser, Maine, USA, 1986 edn.

Daniel, Glyn (ed.) - *'The Illustrated Encyclopedia of Archaeology'*, Macmillan, London, 1978.

Day, Harvey - *'The Hidden Power of Vibrations'*, Sphere, London, 1980.

Desroches-Noblecourt, Christiane - *'Tutankhamen'*, Penguin, London, 1965.

Farrar, Janet and Stewart - *'Spells and How they Work'*, Robert Hale, London, 1991.

Fortune, Dion - *'The Mystical Qabalah'*, Aquarian Press, Northants., 1987.

Fortune, Dion - *'Applied Magic'*, Aquarian, Northants, 1987.

Gantz, Jeffrey (trans.) - *'The Mabinogion'*, Penguin, London, 1976.

Gettings, Fred - *'Encyclopedia of the Occult'*, Rider, London, 1986.

Gimbutas, Marija - *'The Goddesses and Gods of Old Europe, 6500 - 3500 BC: Myths and Cult Images'*, Thames and Hudson, 1982.

Gimbutas, Marija - *'The Language of the Goddess'*, Thames & Hudson, London, 1989.

Glover, T R - *'The Ancient World'*, Pelican, Middx, 1944.

Graves, Robert - *'The White Goddess'*, Faber & Faber, London, 1961.
Guerber, H A - *'Greece and Rome: Myths and Legends'*, Senate, London, 1994.
Guerber, H A - *'The Norsemen'*, Senate, London, 1994.
Guest, Charlotte - *'Mabinogion Legends'*, Llanerch, Felinfach, 1992.
Hart, George - *'Egyptian Gods and Goddesses'*, Routledge, London, 1986.
Hope, Murry - *'Practical Egyptian Magic'*, Aquarian Press, Northants., 1984.
Hope, Murry - *'Practical Celtic Magic'*, Aquarian Press, Northants., 1987.
Howard, Michael - *'Understanding Runes'*, Aquarian Press, Northants, 1990. New version published as *'Mysteries of the Runes'*, Capall Bann 1994
Humphrey, Naomi - *'Meditation: the Inner Way'*, Aquarian, Northants., 1987.
King, Bernard - *'The Runes'*, Element, Dorset, 1993.
Larousse - *'New Encyclopedia of Mythology'*, Paul Hamlyn, London, 1968.
MacGregor-Mathers, S L - *'The Book of the Sacred Magic of Abra-Melin the Mage'*, Aquarian, Northants, 1976.
Matthews, Caitlin - *'The Celtic Tradition'*, Element, Dorset, 1989.
Megaw, Ruth and Vincent - *'Early Celtic Art'*, Shire, Bucks, 1986.
McCrone, John - *'The Ape that Spoke: Language and the Evolution of the Human Mind'*, Picador, Pan Books, London, 1991.
Meaden, George Terence - *'The Goddess of the Stones'*, Souvenir Press, London, 1991.
Murray, Liz and Colin - *'The Celtic Tree Oracle'*, Rider, London, 1988.
Pálsson, Herman and Edwards, Paul (trans.) - *'Egil's Saga'*, Penguin, London, 1976.
Pennick, Nigel - *'The Secret Lore of Runes and Other Ancient Alphabets'*, Rider, London, 1991.
Percy, Thomas - *'Reliques of Ancient English Poetry'*, Swan Sonnenschein & Co, London, 1891.
Reed, Ellen Cannon - 'Invocation of the Gods: Ancient Egyptian Magic for Today', Llewellyn, Minnesota, USA, 1992.
Rolleston, T W - *'Celtic Myths and Legends'*, Bracken Books, London.
Romer, John - *'People of the Nile'*, Michael Joseph, London, 1989.
Rutherford, Ward - *'The Druids: Magicians of the West'*, Aquarian Press, Northants., 1978.
Stewart, R J - *'Celtic Gods, Celtic Goddesses'*, Blandford, London, 1990.
Thorsson, Edred - *'Runelore'*, Samuel Weiser, Maine, USA, 1987.
Twohig, Elizabeth Shee - *'Irish Megalithic Tombs'*, Shire, Bucks, 1990.
Wilson, Colin - *'The Occult'*, Grafton, London, 1979.

Index

Abraham 49, 59
Abraham the Jew 184
Abramelin the Mage, The Book of
the Sacred Magic of 181-184
Adad 59
Æsir 150, 153
Ættir 162
Agrippa, Cornelius 179
Akkadian language 47, 52
Amergin 90
Angles 140
Anglo-Saxon Futhork 145, 158,
159, 162, 165
Anglo-Saxon Rune Poem 159, 165
Ankh 21, 31, 32, 72, 129
An-Ki 57
Apep 34
Apollo 119, 127, 129
Apollonian Script 179
Apollonius of Tyana 179
Aramaic alphabet 115
Aramaic language 52
Arianrhod 110
Arthurian tales 84,102
Asgard 151
Ask 152
Assyria 47, 52
Assyrian language 52
Attic dialect 112
Automatic writing 190
Avalon 102
Awen 105, 107, 108, 188

Babylon/Babylonia 46, 47, 49, 51
Babylonian language 52
Balder 157
Barddas 105, 107
Bardic belief 105-109

Bards 2, 79-93, 102
Basque language 15
Bath 135, 136
Battle of the Trees 88
Bede 156
Bel 59
Bible 2, 20, 54, 76
Bind-rune 163, 174
Birds of Rhiannon 81
Bligh Bond, Frederick 191-192
Boden 153
Book of Ballymote 93, 97
Book of the Dead, Egyptian 37,
38, 39
Book of Invasions 79, 80, 84, 90
Book of Taliesin 88
Brahma 187
Bran 100, 109
Branwen, Daughter of Llyr 100
Bres 80
Breton language 79
Bride 91
Brunler, Oscar 187
Brythonic language 78, 79

Cad Goddeu 88, 95, 109
Cadmus 116, 117
Caduceus 119, 121
Canaan 49, 50
Celestial Script 179
Celtic language 16, 78
Celts 75-78
Ceremonial magic 179
Ceridwen 86-88
Cervantes 195
Champollion, Jean Franáois 30
Charms of the Bards 108
Chatres Cathedral 122

Chi-Rho symbol 129, 131
Chladni, Ernst 3
ChrÇtien de Troyes 84
Christ 123, 127, 129, 131
Christianity 123, 125, 129, 131,
   136, 140, 141, 145
Coelbren 107-109
Coelvain 109
Coptic, dialect and script 29
Cornish language 79
Crane 117, 119
Crowley, Aleister 177
Cuchulainn 77, 97, 109, 111
Cuneiform 51, 52
Curses 135, 158
Cyrus 49, 51

Dee, Dr John 177
Demotic script 29, 30
Dindsenchas 110
Dionysus 103, 119
Djeheuty 23, 27
Druidry 78, 85
Druids 75, 79, 81, 100, 101, 109
Duat 25, 37, 38, 39

Ebillion 108
Ego 8
Egypt 11, 15, 16, 18-42, 49, 55,
   104
Egyptian Book of the Dead 37,
   38, 39
Einigan the Giant 107
Eisteddfod 86
Elder Edda 147
Elder Futhark 145, 156, 159,
   162, 165
Elphin 87
Embla 152
English language 16, 17, 112,
   139, 141
Enlil 57

Enochian alphabet 175, 177
Epic literature 113
Epicharmus 117
Erik Bloodaxe 155-156
Erin 90
Etruscan culture 113,115, 119
Etruscan script 115, 141, 143

Fáith (Fáithi) 81
Fates 117, 120, 125, 126
Fili (Filid) 81, 83
Fianna 89
Finn MacCumhaill 89, 102, 109
Finneces 89
Fintan 89, 102
Fortune, Dion 188
Freemasonry 21, 127, 181

Gaelic alphabet 99
Gaelic language 78, 79
Gaul 75, 79
Gavreau, Professor 186
Geis 97
Gematria (Greek) 121-131
Gematria (Hebrew) 56, 72-74
Genesis 54, 55, 68
Geraint Vardd Glas 108
Gerald of Wales 111
German language 141
Gilgamesh, Epic of 52
Gnostic belief 122
Golden Section 122, 125, 127, 129
Gothic language 140, 141, 143
Goths 140, 141
Graphology 192
Graves, Robert 95, 100, 104, 105
Greek alphabet 75, 112, 115-119,
   121-131, 141
Greek culture 112-113
Greek language 115
Grim 149
Grimoire 3, 175

Grimoire of Honorius 179
Group mind 188-189
Gunhild 155-156
Gunlod 153
Gungnir 150, 152
Gwern 100
Gwion Bach 87
Gwydion 109, 110

Hall of Two Truths 25
HÑllristningar symbols 143
Hallstatt culture 77
Hammurabi 47, 52
Hatshepsut 36
H†v†mal 147,160
Heavenly Script 179
Hebrew alphabet 51, 52, 54, 63-
 74, 115
Hebrew language 30, 52, 55
Hebrews 46, 47, 49, 50, 51
Heimskringla 147
Hel 151
Heliopolis 33
Hermes 117, 119, 129
Hermes Trismegistos 27, 119-120
Hermetic Cannon 120, 122
Hermopolis 20
Herodotus 112, 116
Heru 32
Hesiod 113
Hesperides 103
Hieratic script   29
Hieroglyphs 27, 30
Hindu belief 187
Hittite language 15
Homer   113
Homeric Hymns 113
Horemheb 37
Horus 32, 40, 125
Hugin 150
Hygenus, Caius Julius 117, 119,
 121

Ibis 23, 119
Iceland 140, 146, 147, 149
Icelandic language 141
Idun 103
Illiad 113
Indo-European languages 15, 16,
 78, 113, 141
Indo-European religion 78
Ionic alphabet 116
Isis 34, 35, 40, 125
Israel 51
Ithel the Tawny 108

Jarl Hakon 154
Jehovah 55, 73
Jemdet Nasr Culture 19
Jenny, Hans 3
Jericho 50
Jerusalem, Temple of 56
Jesus 104, 129
Jones, William   15
Joseph 49
Joshua   50
Judah 49, 51
Julius Ceasar 75, 140, 164, 165

Key of Solomon 179
Kelley, Edward 177
Khepera 20, 31, 32, 39, 46
Kvasir 153

Lakhovsky, George 185
Language, History of 6-10
Language, Power of 188-190
Lascaux cave 10
La Téne culture 77
Latin language 15, 16, 17, 76,
 141
Latin alphabet 99, 108, 137-
 138, 141
Llew 110
Lugh 79

Maat 32, 38
Maati, Hall of 37, 38
Mabinogion 85, 86
MacGregor Mathers, S.L. 181
Magical squares 181, 184
Malachim Script 175
Mantras 2, 3, 187
Marduk 59
Memphis 19, 21, 40
Menes 19
Menw the Aged 107
Mercury 119
Mesopotamia 47, 49, 51
Midgard 151
Milesians 90, 91
Mimir 150
Minoan culture 112
Minoan scripts 113
Minstrels 83, 84, 85
Morganwg, Iolo 86, 105
Moses 49, 55, 56
Moses de Leon 59
Mount Sinai 50
Munin 150
Muses 120
Mycenean culture 112, 113

Name 9, 10, 33-34, 35, 36, 38, 54,
    107, 109, 131, 179-180
Nammu 56, 68
Neb-er-tcher 20
Nebuchadnezzar II 51
Nennius 111
Newgrange 11
New Testament 115, 122
Norman French 17
Norns 151, 164, 170
Norse literature 146, 147, 149
Norse mythology 152
Norwegians 140
Notarikon 72, 74
Numerology, Western 131-135

Numerology, Runic 163

Odhroerir 153
Odin 139, 147, 149-154, 157, 158,
    160, 169, 171, 173
Odyssey 113, 115
Oghma 89, 91-93
Ogham 91, 93-105
Oisin 89
Ollamhs 81-84
Old English language 141, 143
Old Europe 13, 15
Old High German language 141,
    143
Old Icelandic Rune Poem 165
Old Norse language 140, 141,
    143, 149
Old Norwegian Rune Rhyme 165
Old Saxon language 141, 143
Old Testament   46, 49, 55
Osiris 25, 27, 38, 40, 125
Ossianic Cycle 85, 89
Otherworld, Celtic 76, 81, 83,
    102, 105
Ovates 79, 81
Owein 88

Palamedes 117
Palladio 121
Papyrus 27, 29
Parthenon 122
Passing the River Script 179
Pathworking 42
Peithynen frame 108
Pelasgian alphabet 117
Pentagram 103, 125
Pepi I 36
Phoenician alphabet 51, 52, 115
Phoenician language 52
Poetic Edda 147
Poetry 194, 198-199
Poet's Share 153

Prose, History of 194
Ptah 18-21, 23, 31-33, 42, 46
Pythagoras 121

Qabalah 54, 56, 59-74, 122, 179

Ra 32-36, 56
Ragnarök 147, 150
Ramesses II 50
Rawlinson, Henry 52
Red Book of Hergest 85, 86
Revelation of St John 123, 147
Rhiannon 110
Ritual 195-196
Roman alphabet 99, 108, 137-138, 141
Roman culture 113-115, 135
Rosecrucian alphabets 181
Rosetta Stone 30
Runatál 147, 150, 151, 156, 160, 161
Runemasters 154-156, 158, 160-161, 164, 192
Rune poems 145, 146, 165, 167-174
Runes 13, 108, 115, 139, 141-147, 150-152, 154-174
Runic divination 164

Sëmund 147
Sagas, Norse 147
St Columba 81
St John 54, 123, 147
Salmon of Wisdom 89, 102
Sanskrit 15, 16
Saul 50
Saxons 140
Scandinavia 140, 141, 145, 146
Scandinavian language 141
Scottish bardic schools 83
Scribes, Egyptian 25
Sciptura Coelestis 179

Sekhmet 23
Sepher Yetzirah 59, 63, 66
Set 40
Setnau 40-42
Shamanism 78, 88, 151, 153, 194
Shelley, Mary 197
Shemahamphorash 56
Shiva 187
Shu 32
Silver Branch 81
Simonides 117, 119
Skalds 147-149, 153
Skallagrimsson, Egil 147, 149, 155
Sleipnir 149, 152, 173
Solomon 50, 51
Son 153
Sonics 80
Sovereign Princes' Rose Cross Cipher 181
Sturluson, Snorri 147
Sumeria 46, 47
Sumerian language 52
Suttung 153
Symbols, Prehistoric 11, 189
Syria 19
Syrian alphabet 115, 116

Tacitus 75, 140, 164, 165
Tain Bo Cuailgne 77, 84, 97
Taliesin 86-88, 108

Talismans 127, 135, 137, 154, 157, 158, 174, 179, 184
Tehuti 23
Temurah 72, 74
Tesla, Nikola 186
Tetragrammaton 55, 62, 67, 68, 107, 123
Teutonic languages 141
Teutonic mythology 140, 146
Teutonic peoples 140, 143

Thorleif 154
Thoth 20, 23, 25, 27, 40, 46, 119, 120
Tiamat 68
Tiw 162
Toland, John 85
Torah 50, 56
Transitus Fluvii Script 179
Tree Alphabet 93-105
Tree Calendar 104, 105
Tree of Knowledge 59
Tree of Life 59-63
Triads, Welsh 85
Troubadours 84
Tuatha de Danaan 79, 90, 93
Tutankhamen 37
Tuthmosis 36

Uley, Temple of 135
Ulster Cycle 84
Unas 39
Ur 47
Urien of Rheged 88

Vanir 150, 153
Vé 152
Vedas 15, 16
Venus of Willendorf 10
Vibration 185-189, 196
Viking Futhork 145, 159, 162, 165
Vili 152
Vishnu 187
Vitruvius 122
Völupsá 147

Well of Segais 89, 102
Welsh language 78, 79
West Germanic tribes 140
White Book of Rhydderch 85
Wild Hunt 149
Williams, Edward 86

Woden 149
Word squares 136, 137
Writing of the Magi 179

Yaweh 54, 56, 59, 63, 72
Yggdrasil (Norse World Tree) 150, 151, 153, 169, 171
Ymir 152
Younger Edda 147
Younger Futhork 145, 159, 162, 165

Zodiac 62, 67
Zohar 59

FREE DETAILED CATALOGUE

Capall Bann is owned and run by people actively involved in many of the areas in which we publish. A detailed illustrated catalogue is available on request, SAE or International Postal Coupon appreciated. **Titles can be ordered direct from Capall Bann, post free in the UK** (cheque or PO with order) or from good bookshops and specialist outlets.

Do contact us for details on the latest releases at: **Capall Bann Publishing, Freshfields, Chieveley, Berks, RG20 8TF.** Titles include:

A Breath Behind Time, Terri Hector
Angels and Goddesses - Celtic Christianity & Paganism, M. Howard
Arthur - The Legend Unveiled, C Johnson & E Lung
Astrology The Inner Eye - A Guide in Everyday Language, E Smith
Auguries and Omens - The Magical Lore of Birds, Yvonne Aburrow
Asyniur - Womens Mysteries in the Northern Tradition, S McGrath
Beginnings - Geomancy, Builder's Rites & Electional Astrology in the
        European Tradition, Nigel Pennick
Between Earth and Sky, Julia Day
Book of the Veil , Peter Paddon
Caer Sidhe - Celtic Astrology and Astronomy, Vol 1, Michael Bayley
Caer Sidhe - Celtic Astrology and Astronomy, Vol 2 M Bayley
Call of the Horned Piper, Nigel Jackson
Cat's Company, Ann Walker
Celtic Faery Shamanism, Catrin James
Celtic Faery Shamanism - The Wisdom of the Otherworld, Catrin James
Celtic Lore & Druidic Ritual, Rhiannon Ryall
Celtic Sacrifice - Pre Christian Ritual & Religion, Marion Pearce
Celtic Saints and the Glastonbury Zodiac, Mary Caine
Circle and the Square, Jack Gale
Compleat Vampyre - The Vampyre Shaman, Nigel Jackson
Creating Form From the Mist - The Wisdom of Women in Celtic Myth and
        Culture, Lynne Sinclair-Wood
Crystal Clear - A Guide to Quartz Crystal, Jennifer Dent
Crystal Doorways, Simon & Sue Lilly
Crossing the Borderlines - Guising, Masking & Ritual Animal Disguise in the
        European Tradition, Nigel Pennick
Dragons of the West, Nigel Pennick
Earth Dance - A Year of Pagan Rituals, Jan Brodie
Earth Harmony - Places of Power, Holiness & Healing, Nigel Pennick
Earth Magic, Margaret McArthur

Eildon Tree (The) Romany Language & Lore, Michael Hoadley
Enchanted Forest - The Magical Lore of Trees, Yvonne Aburrow
Eternal Priestess, Sage Weston
Eternally Yours Faithfully, Roy Radford & Evelyn Gregory
Everything You Always Wanted To Know About Your Body, But So Far
    Nobody's Been Able To Tell You, Chris Thomas & D Baker
Face of the Deep - Healing Body & Soul, Penny Allen
Fairies in the Irish Tradition, Molly Gowen
Familiars - Animal Powers of Britain, Anna Franklin
Fool's First Steps, (The) Chris Thomas
Forest Paths - Tree Divination, Brian Harrison, Ill. S. Rouse
From Past to Future Life, Dr Roger Webber
Gardening For Wildlife Ron Wilson
God Year, The, Nigel Pennick & Helen Field
Goddess on the Cross, Dr George Young
Goddess Year, The, Nigel Pennick & Helen Field
Goddesses, Guardians & Groves, Jack Gale
Handbook For Pagan Healers, Liz Joan
Handbook of Fairies, Ronan Coghlan
Healing Book, The, Chris Thomas and Diane Baker
Healing Homes, Jennifer Dent
Healing Journeys, Paul Williamson
Healing Stones, Sue Philips
Herb Craft - Shamanic & Ritual Use of Herbs, Lavender & Franklin
Hidden Heritage - Exploring Ancient Essex, Terry Johnson
Hub of the Wheel, Skytoucher
In Search of Herne the Hunter, Eric Fitch
Inner Celtia, Alan Richardson & David Annwn
Inner Mysteries of the Goths, Nigel Pennick
Inner Space Workbook - Develop Thru Tarot, C Summers & J Vayne
Intuitive Journey, Ann Walker Isis - African Queen, Akkadia Ford
Journey Home, The, Chris Thomas
Kecks, Keddles & Kesh - Celtic Lang & The Cog Almanac, Bayley
Language of the Psycards, Berenice
Legend of Robin Hood, The, Richard Rutherford-Moore
Lid Off the Cauldron, Patricia Crowther
Light From the Shadows - Modern Traditional Witchcraft, Gwyn
Living Tarot, Ann Walker
Lore of the Sacred Horse, Marion Davies
Lost Lands & Sunken Cities (2nd ed.), Nigel Pennick
Magic of Herbs - A Complete Home Herbal, Rhiannon Ryall
Magical Guardians - Exploring the Spirit and Nature of Trees, Philip Heselton
Magical History of the Horse, Janet Farrar & Virginia Russell
Magical Lore of Animals, Yvonne Aburrow
Magical Lore of Cats, Marion Davies
Magical Lore of Herbs, Marion Davies

210

Magick Without Peers, Ariadne Rainbird & David Rankine
Masks of Misrule - Horned God & His Cult in Europe, Nigel Jackson
Medicine For The Coming Age, Lisa Sand MD
Medium Rare - Reminiscences of a Clairvoyant, Muriel Renard
Menopausal Woman on the Run, Jaki da Costa
Mind Massage - 60 Creative Visualisations, Marlene Maundrill
Mirrors of Magic - Evoking the Spirit of the Dewponds, P Heselton
Moon Mysteries, Jan Brodie
Mysteries of the Runes, Michael Howard
Mystic Life of Animals, Ann Walker
New Celtic Oracle The, Nigel Pennick & Nigel Jackson
Oracle of Geomancy, Nigel Pennick
Pagan Feasts - Seasonal Food for the 8 Festivals, Franklin & Phillips
Patchwork of Magic - Living in a Pagan World, Julia Day
Pathworking - A Practical Book of Guided Meditations, Pete Jennings
Personal Power, Anna Franklin
Pickingill Papers - The Origins of Gardnerian Wicca, Bill Liddell
Pillars of Tubal Cain, Nigel Jackson
Places of Pilgrimage and Healing, Adrian Cooper
Practical Divining, Richard Foord
Practical Meditation, Steve Hounsome
Practical Spirituality, Steve Hounsome
Psychic Self Defence - Real Solutions, Jan Brodie
Real Fairies, David Tame
Reality - How It Works & Why It Mostly Doesn't, Rik Dent
Romany Tapestry, Michael Houghton
Runic Astrology, Nigel Pennick
Sacred Animals, Gordon MacLellan
Sacred Celtic Animals, Marion Davies, Ill. Simon Rouse
Sacred Dorset - On the Path of the Dragon, Peter Knight
Sacred Grove - The Mysteries of the Forest, Yvonne Aburrow
Sacred Geometry, Nigel Pennick
Sacred Nature, Ancient Wisdom & Modern Meanings, A Cooper
Sacred Ring - Pagan Origins of British Folk Festivals, M. Howard
Season of Sorcery - On Becoming a Wisewoman, Poppy Palin
Seasonal Magic - Diary of a Village Witch, Paddy Slade
Secret Places of the Goddess, Philip Heselton
Secret Signs & Sigils, Nigel Pennick
Self Enlightenment, Mayan O'Brien
Spirits of the Air, Jaq D Hawkins
Spirits of the Earth, Jaq D Hawkins
Spirits of the Water, Jaq D Hawkins
Spirits of the Fire, Jaq D Hawkins
Spirits of the Aether, Jaq D Hawkins
Stony Gaze, Investigating Celtic Heads John Billingsley
Stumbling Through the Undergrowth , Mark Kirwan-Heyhoe

Subterranean Kingdom, The, revised 2nd ed, Nigel Pennick
Symbols of Ancient Gods, Rhiannon Ryall
Talking to the Earth, Gordon MacLellan
Taming the Wolf - Full Moon Meditations, Steve Hounsome
Teachings of the Wisewomen, Rhiannon Ryall
The Other Kingdoms Speak, Helena Hawley
Tree: Essence of Healing, Simon & Sue Lilly
Tree: Essence, Spirit & Teacher, Simon & Sue Lilly
Through the Veil, Peter Paddon
Torch and the Spear, Patrick Regan
Understanding Chaos Magic, Jaq D Hawkins
Vortex - The End of History, Mary Russell
Warp and Weft - In Search of the I-Ching, William de Fancourt
Warriors at the Edge of Time, Jan Fry
Water Witches, Tony Steele
Way of the Magus, Michael Howard
Weaving a Web of Magic, Rhiannon Ryall
West Country Wicca, Rhiannon Ryall
Wildwitch - The Craft of the Natural Psychic, Poppy Palin
Wildwood King , Philip Kane
Witches of Oz, Matthew & Julia Philips
Wondrous Land - The Faery Faith of Ireland by Dr Kay Mullin
Working With the Merlin, Geoff Hughes
Your Talking Pet, Ann Walker

FREE detailed catalogue and FREE 'Inspiration' magazine

Contact: Capall Bann Publishing, Freshfields, Chieveley, Berks, RG20 8TF